D1708255

DISSENT DENIED
The Technocratic Response
to Protest

Marlis Krueger / Frieda Silvert

DISSENT DENIED

The Technocratic Response to Protest

ELSEVIER

New York / Oxford / Amsterdam

ELSEVIER SCIENTIFIC PUBLISHING COMPANY, INC.
52 Vanderbilt Avenue, New York, N.Y. 10017

ELSEVIER SCIENTIFIC PUBLISHING COMPANY
335 Jan Van Galenstraat, P.O. Box 211
Amsterdam, The Netherlands

Library of Congress Cataloging in Publication Data

Krüger, Marlis.
  Dissent denied.

  Includes index.
  1. Radicalism—United States.   2.   United States—
Social conditions—1960-   3.   College students—
United States—Political activity.   I.   Silvert, Frieda,
joint author.   II.   Title.
HN90.R3K78   322.4′4′0973   75-8273
ISBN 0-444-99005-4

Manufactured in the United States of America

Contents

Preface

Since this book was conceived, the tumultuous and exuberant political climate of the sixties has changed to one of calculated caution and economic fear. But the mid-seventies' new psychological state and economic constellation are not disconnected from the critiques voiced on the campuses and in the streets by students and blacks. The long days' night of Watergate was the watershed. Protest is now both subterranean and all-encompassing. There is the danger, however, that anxiety over economic survival will blur issues once clarified and diffuse organized protest; that the political learning process, begun in the sixties, may thus be undone and the connections made between individual experiences and society at large dissociated.

The political socialization of a generation, however, cannot be so easily destroyed or countermanded. To off-set its social criticism would require strong and conscious efforts on the part of those interested in the status quo so long as American society is based on inequality and inequity.

At present, economic recession and the national leadership's political disorientation runs a contrapuntal theme with new expressions of dissent and protest. Congressmen now question the once sacrosanct requests of a Secretary of Defense and demand accountability from the Department of Defense. They have even looked into their own house and have already surprised the public with the swiftness of certain changes. Women and ethnic groups now review the rules and rationale behind hiring and firing procedures. Union and consumer action groups are digging deep into the once unknown regions of capital accumulation and investment policies of corporations, banks, and the government. While the grumblings of dissent are now everywhere, one former center of visible confrontation — the university — appears quiet and accommodating. Today, universities are financially hard-pressed and the academic community is beginning to rationalize the inadequacy of its performance. This book explores the sources of the university's acquiescence to the economic necessity of limiting its potential to create alternative modes of thought. During the sixties, the universities were in the paradoxical position of being both the locus of critical dissent because of their emphasis on scientific inquiry and the home of ideological paradigms designed to limit or destroy its critical potential. The paradox has become more clouded in the mid-seventies. Academia's inefficacious performance is now being excused on the basis of the scarcity of funds, and, of course, there is some honesty in this. But the better part of truth lies in the fact that academics tend to be captives of their own apologetic machinations, persistent in their refusal to risk the discomfort of critical reflection and open intellectual debate.

Since we are members of the academic community, we have been subject to the constraints of the paradox. This book is, thus, also our effort to come to terms with the dilemmas resulting from the dialectics between academe and society. We leave it to the reader to judge how well we have succeeded in breaking the limitations of the current intellectual constellation in the social sciences.

New York City   M.K.
March 1975   F.M.S.

Acknowledgements

In writing this book, we encountered many obstacles which were due not only to the usual difficulties of collaboration, but also to the disparity in cultural and life experiences. We have a feeling of satisfaction that we have bridged our differences in personality, style, age, socio-cultural background, professional training, political persuasion, and possibly Weltanschauung. We spent many hours arguing about concepts and even words. As we went along, each of us changed her perspective. We are not sure, however, if we did not also make some compromises — contrary to our intention — for practical purposes. Be this as it may, we have learned from each other and have been able to objectify our thought processes, discussions, and exchange. Since influence and learning have been mutual and equal, the prevalent professional principle of senior and junior authorship does not apply to this book. Our structured conversations on the forms and possibilities of change and dissent in the United States and the state of the social sciences ended in the Fall of 1973.

We would like to thank in particular Bärbel Wallisch-Prinz and Kalman Silvert who, in one way or another, helped us to stay with our project. Many of our former students at CCNY played important roles in various phases of our work by their very presence, intellectual stimulation and empirical research assistance. Our special thanks go to Gaby Lipshutz, Nancy Naito, Marlies Gluck, Alexander Rosenzweig and Cathy Remy. Their specific labors will be more evident in another book.

Arthur Paris and Paget Henry read an earlier draft of the manuscript and provided constructive comments on the chapter about black student protest. Norman Birnbaum, Leonard Reissman, David Muchnick and John Semack also offered valuable criticism of various sections. Finally, we want to thank our editor, William Gum, for his help in turning the manuscript into a book.

PART

I

UNIVERSITIES AND GHETTOES

1
THEMES
AND THESES

I

The vulgarity and waste of racism, inequality, and apologetics continue to distort the national interest in the nineteen-seventies. Looking backward to the sixties, when these distortions were so explicitly and, at times, so violently exposed by blacks and students, one is given to ask why the successes of dissent were so incomplete, so bitter. Can it be that the bitterness springs from utopian passions—said to fuel the critical spirit—which refuse to die? Now that the conspiracy of deception lying beneath the Watergate affair has become an open secret, we are invited to question whether the social science soothsayers—who declared an end to ideology in the early sixties—were belied not only by the young and the black, but also by a governmental passion to betray the democratic ethos. Can it be that bitterness is difficult to assuage when incomplete successes turn into unbenign failures?

There are persons who hope the bitterness will pass, who insist that the just demands of the protest movement will be made a part of the American conscience. The necessarily brutal measures used to quell protesters' excesses, they say, will be forgiven and illegitimate issues forgotten once realities overcome idealistic passions. Then there are those who say it is too soon to tell whether the protest

3

movement is done and gone. They point to the bitterness that keeps surfacing to warn us that we enjoy only an uneasy peace. Dissent has many styles and varied uses, and the consequences of one affect the other. Whether protest continues or dies, they say, is subject to the play of consequences only now making themselves felt.

Certainly one lesson was well learned during the sixties—the acceptable limits and direct costs of passionate opposition. Black students learned it in the deaths of their brothers at Jackson State College, and white students learned it at Kent State. Not as deadly dramatic, but equally crucial is another lesson learned: the inequalities of race and sex, the democratic participation in policy decisions, and the distribution of goods and services in an economy of technical abundance demand either a qualitative reordering of priorities to eliminate such inequalities or oppressive measures to ensure their continuance. A related lesson, but less understood, is the pertinence of intellectuals, academics, and the university to the ideological battle being waged over these alternatives. Academics and intellectuals equipped with political slogans and manning the battle stations, have begun to take their stands. Some are the "new conservatives"—liberal cold warriors of yesteryear who now defend the *status quo* and the necessity of uncompromising "law and order." The new conservatives reject the critical task of exploring the real possibilities of full equality and authentic freedom, although for the first time in history, the technical and productive means for the liberation so yearned for have become available. Instead, they are ready to extol the virtues of order in the "coming technocratic culture." Other intellectuals follow the banner of the "new radicalism," reaffirming their dedication to the "critical spirit" and the dialectical imagination which they hope will combine the possibilities of reason with enlightened practice. Neither side is yet consolidated in opinion or number, and each group's margin fades into that middle ground where academics and intellectuals, like their compatriots outside the university, wait and see, dispassionate or numbed, continually surprised by the turn of events.

The themes of this book have to do with the second and third lessons: the effects of inequality and the structural relationship of intellectuals to it. Why these themes? Because we think they join

4

two contradictory tendencies of American society: the struggle to attain equality for all—in which the creative talent and thoughts of intellectuals and scientists supposedly have been enlisted—and the opposing forces, real and imagined, which abort its fulfillment. And we are interested in intellectuals not only because theirs were among the loudest protest voices in the sixties, but also because as their labors become visibly important for our society, they are being pushed more and more to the core of the contradiction. In Chapters Three to Seven we dissect the products of these beleaguered intellectuals.

It has become more than abundantly clear; the protests of students and the attacks on the university were not by chance. Students, if they did not "know" of the trend to growing oppression, "felt" it, and dissented. Blacks and the urban poor, if they knew nothing of the rationalizations and theories being prepared for the legitimation of their exclusion from society, "felt" and "lived" the effects of social policies derived from these "intellectual" under-standings. And *they* dissented. Understanding the working out of these dissents requires a critical assessment of the interplay of the sources of policy formation and policy decision-making, and the interconnectedness of the university and the state.

Our cooperative effort is the result of a confluence of our long-standing theoretical interest in the possibilities of qualitative change in advanced capitalist societies and the impact of a protest incident in our immediate professional environment. Personal histories and a curiosity about cross-cultural scholarly cooperation provided the readiness to put the two together.

The incident was the take-over of New York's City College South Campus by black and Puerto Rican students in April, 1969. In the days that followed, the social-science faculty divided, as had happened on so many other campuses, into those who took to personal retreat and those who became partisans. For those of us who stayed, the vicissitudes of the conflict and its politics became a way of life for many months and, of course, took their toll on both sides of the line.

The month of May was difficult. But in the midst of the myriad vacillations between this or that strategy or tactic, the noise and the confusion—in one of those deadening anticlimactic lulls which occur even in the worst of confrontations—professional curiosity piqued us, and the idea of this study was born. Our initial purpose was to reconstruct the take-over and assess its meaning for the college community. But we soon realized that individual protest events were tied to broader structural conditions and other manifestations of unrest. Our research therefore aimed at the conceptualization of the protest scene as a concrete whole as well as the detailed analysis of the confrontation at City College.* This book presents our attempt to comprehend the protest of the sixties, and we leave the assessment of the local incident for another volume.

We are aware that there is a difference between the method of investigation and the method of presentation. The first, being subject to the uneven process and changing interplay between theoretical concerns and procedural needs, is always constrained by technical conditions. The second, in our view, demands the infusion and imposition of a logical structure and order upon the material, because presentation involves communication with others. Both methods, however, are guided by theoretical principles as well as cognitive and political interests, which to a great extent reflect themes and approaches espoused by the sociological tradition.

Sociology was born in an era of political turmoil and socioeconomic crises afflicting early nineteenth-century European society. At that time, scientists concerned with the study of "society" were motivated by different political and cognitive perspectives. Some wanted to reestablish a stable social order for the bourgeoisie based on a newly agreed-upon consensus of ideas that would eradicate the "intellectual anarchy" of their era and give leading authority to the scientific principles of positivism; others wanted to destroy bourgeois society and to replace it with a social organization based on cooperation, equality, self-determination, and the maximum fulfillment of human potential. Accordingly, the latter group conceived of their science as a necessarily critical one. As social scientists, they attempted to identify those tendencies in bourgeois society which would eventually explode and transform it. Thus, the

---

* The intermeshing of micro- and macro-levels of analysis has found a correlate in our alternating use of empirical investigation of details, method of abstraction, and reconstruction of interrelated processes on the level of concrete totality.[1]

existing society was not merely described by them as it was, and thereby scientifically confirmed, but criticized in the light of a future utopia. This utopia, the second group maintained, was a real possibility in the old social order and could be projected on the basis of an extrapolation of the actual socioeconomic disintegrative tendencies of bourgeois society.

Neither Comte nor Marx pursued their scientific studies *l'art pour l'art.* For both social theory and social practice were intricately intertwined even if for opposing purposes. For Comte it was to provide legitimations of early bourgeois society, and thereby increase its stability; and for Marx, to destroy intellectual and cultural justifications (ideologies) and give a scientific orientation to those engaged in a revolutionary struggle.*

These two traditions are still with us. The Comtean contention has developed into an almost monopolistic espousal of positivism in the social sciences. On the societal level, too, we are witnessing the fantastic growth of a quasi-monopoly of technocratic, scientifically justified decisions and planning, and a near belief in the autonomy of science and technology. Marxian analysis, on the other hand, after an aborted flowering during the thirties,† has only recently been reintroduced to the American social-science scene as a countervailing mode to positivism. In the real world, the Marxian thesis has always found empirical referents in economic crises, wars, strikes, riots, and people's protests.

Student protest in a technically highly developed society such as the United States touches on crucial connectives found in both

* Auguste Comte and Karl Marx are ideal-typical representatives of these two positions.

† Although socialism in one form or another was the banner around which artists, actors, humanists, and an important school of reinterpreters of American history had rallied since the latter part of the nineteenth century, Marxism in the nineteen-thirties was considered a point of view rather than a subject of theory. Americans leaned heavily on British social thinkers (John Strachey, R.P. Dutt, Beatrice and Sidney Webb, etc.), and for some very few people, on the careful study of Marx and Lenin. The *New Masses* was the house organ of Marxist intellectual thought and action interpreting the American experience. In the student movement, Joseph Lash and James Wechsler served as principal leaders and "theoreticians." Home-grown Marxist intellectuals like Paul Sweezy and Harold Aptheker were not to produce their major works until the early forties. Recently, a number of translations from the German and French have introduced younger members of the Frankfurt School of Sociology like Jürgen Habermas and Alfred Wellmer, as well as works by Ernest Mandel and Louis Althusser. For the reception of the Frankfurt School on this side of the Atlantic, see, for example, *Continuum*, VIII, Nos. 1 and 2 (Spring-Summer, 1970), and the *Berkeley Journal of Sociology*, XVI (1972), 94ff.

theoretical perspectives. To social scientists it poses a special concern, for they cannot avoid its implications and must seek explanations for its causes, which in turn calls into question the consequences and potency of their theoretical frameworks. Willy-nilly, they find themselves confronted and challenged in their political stances and status positions. That is, the real situation and their theoretical perspectives are barely separable, making the transgressions from "analysis" to "apology" and other forms of distorted interpretation easier than ever. But even when there is no immediate or overt challenge, social scientists are always affected by a fundamental epistemological difficulty which all too often infuses their analyses with ideological elements. The difficulty turns on the problem that historical and social events and processes cannot be "known" as "pure" facts, that they are accessible and comprehensible only if theoretically interpreted from a certain perspective which must be adequate to the real situation. To answer to its own necessities and purposes, then, social-science theory must not only describe and explain an objectively given social reality and its movements, but must at the same time reflect upon its own sociohistorical origins and anticipate its possible application in society. Social reality as the subject matter of theory and the theoretical process itself are thus bound together, because both are part of the same societal totality,[2] although representing different moments of it.

In order to contain these epistemological difficulties in our study of the sixties, we have consciously attempted to analyze student and racial protest as "real" phenomena. We apply the same criterion to the theories about them as well as our own efforts, for all three are interconnected albeit contradictory moments of present-day U.S. society.* The fact that one of us is not an American and has lived in the country for only five years does not alter this nexus. The cultural marginality of one author may have introduced (and we certainly hope it has) an element of distance and relativity into our analysis, but it had to be counterbalanced by intensive study, experience, and active participation in American life, society, and culture by both in

---

* Of course, some readers might argue that ours is a "forced" perspective not shared by all "academic" social scientists.

order to lead to meaningful questions and an "understanding" of the situation.[3]

Our study contains a critical analysis of the available social-scientific theories of black and white student protest, with special reference to their function as justifications of the political *status quo*, and an essayistic interpretation of the historical development and context of radical leftist protest and dissent in the United States. The last chapter assesses the sociopolitical significance of the protest movement and gives a perspective on the present state of "radical dissent."

II

Marginality and Class: A Preliminary Statement

Student protest and intellectuals, racial riots and ethnic minority groups were forced into the public limelight in the sixties and early seventies. On the surface they seemed unrelated, because intellectuals—especially those categorized as professionals—rank high in terms of income, education, prestige, and job satisfaction, while members of ethnic minority groups are usually found at the bottom of the occupational hierarchy. Made up largely of semi-skilled and unskilled workers and the least educated, these marginal groups display a high degree of discontent, political alienation, delinquency, drug and alcohol addiction, as well as physical and mental disease.[4] And yet, the top (students as well as enlightened professionals) and the bottom (ethnic and racial minorities, the unemployed and unemployables) appeared closer together than apart when they entered into temporary coalitions during the sixties. In essence, however, the two protesting groups, which seemingly represented a newly emerged potential for substantive change in the U.S., especially after the blandness of the "cool and uncommitted" fifties, were even closer together than it would appear. They were, in effect, merely different manifestations of unresolved conflicts and recurrent crises that characterize the period of late capitalism. But to analyze the two protest phenomena as related to the same contradictions does not mean to say that they

9

would have the same social significance for a possible transformation of this country. On the contrary, any understanding of the potential that students and intellectuals and/or racial and ethnic minorities might have for changing the American system can be arrived at only if the current state of consciousness, the power base, and the likely development of both are analyzed separately, as well as conjointly, in the context of the total society. Only then can one make some judgment of their radical force.

Intellectuals versus Technocrats

The question of the role of the intellectual in society, particularly the place of the social scientist, has been one of the eternal themes of sociological theorizing since its official beginnings with Comte's vision of the "positive" society governed by sociologically trained planners and moralists—"the cultivators of Positive Science."

Since then, there has been no agreement among social scientists or intellectuals (And who else but intellectuals would concern themselves with this problem?) about who or what an intellectual is. More often than not, this disquieting lack of agreement is due to the fact that the very people setting out to answer the question are part of the problem. "Whether one calls it 'critical distance,' 'detachment,' or 'objectivity,' none of these principles seems fully guaranteed when intellectuals set out to view themselves,"[5] although they may be motivated by the best of intentions.

The crux of the controversy seems to be whether the definition of the "intellectual" should be normative in character or not.* From a normative point of view, intellectuals have been defined as social critics, dissenters, "counter-experts in the business of defining reality,"[6] or synthesizers of conflicting ideologies.[7] These conceptions imply that intellectuals are socially marginal, unattached, or "free-floating."[8] From the analytical point of view, the suggestion has been that intellectuals should be defined in terms of their activities regardless of the political consequences and moral implications of their work. Intellectual activity, for its part, is

* The definition is also complicated by the fact that various terms —"men of ideas," "scientists," "academics," "professionals," "intelligentsia"—are used interchangeably to differentiate intellectuals from other groups.

relegated to the creation, distribution, and application of culture,[9] while the cultural realm itself tends to be reserved for artists, philosophers, social theorists, and the faculties of university liberal arts departments. Science and technology, in this view, do not lend themselves to such "genuine" intellectual activity and are generally counted among the productive forces. Thus, in the process of defining "intellectual" work, the analytical approach takes on a normative coloration. To the extent that both sides to the controversy—the social-critic theorists and the analytical thinkers—place intellectuals outside the world of production, there is little difference between them. This singular linkage between culture-creation and "intellectuality" is not only obsolete but questionable, because it accepts at face value the inevitability of the historical development of the sciences and disciplines.[10]

A third, more recent position has added yet another dimension to the dispute and found some followers, especially among phe-nomenologically and ethnomethodologically oriented sociologists.[11] Taking off from George Herbert Mead's early contention[12] that one could hardly discern a difference between the attempts on the part of common-sense people to control rationally their everyday world and intellectual scientific activity, this group of social scientists has tried to illuminate the interwoven character of daily existence and the articulation of ideas. The shift of focus suggested by the phenomenological school and attempts to apply a sociology-of-knowledge perspective to the place of intellectuals[13] has not lowered the level of controversy. The dispute still revolves around the questions whether an intellectual is (should be) apologist for, critic, or neutral observer of his society; whether the label "intellectual" is (should be) reserved for the "cultural" or "purely theoretical" disciplines or should also be extended to the applied sciences; whether intellectuals are (should be) institutionally bound (e.g., in universities, academies) and finally, whether intellectuals remain (should remain) purely theoretical, that is, aloof from praxis and the political power play or whether they are (should be) engaged in social and political practice.

It is these questions which are the backdrop of the following discussion. We will argue that "intellectuality" *generally* should be

11

defined as a human potential of critical reflection about the origins and usages of one's work in a given society. Intellectuality does not refer to abstract speculation. Rather, the intellectual act is always mediated through labor, while an "idea" is both product and initiator of the work process. This also applies to modern capitalist societies, even though the split between physical and mental labor has reached the point where whole realms of intellectual activities are viewed as self-sustaining entities, apparently dissociated from, and even antithetical to, the production sector. In such societies, however, there is a simultaneous and crucial process, translating—as it does with all other work—the product-character of an "idea" into the condition of being a commodity. We must recognize the existing division between people who are more involved in cerebral activity* as opposed to those engaged in physical, "senseless"† work. But we must see, also, that both groups are produced by and living in an alienated society. Type of labor, however, does not limit the critical capacity to any one group, for critical reflection remains a universal human potential, although the chances of its realization are not randomly distributed.

The critical component of intellectual potential takes on crucial importance in advanced capitalism, we would argue, because it would open the road toward erasing the false differentiation within labor and, with the restoration of unity, permit the possibility of destroying the deceptive image of an atomized society. In this book we deal with specific groups in order to ascertain the extent of critical potential enabling them to transcend their alienating circumstances. The groups are students, representatives of the "intellectual" sector, and ascribed minority groups (particularly, blacks), because they were the principals involved in the protests of the sixties. In our use of the term "intellectuals" we take into account the historical development of the division of labor, and when applying it to "students," we are cognizant of its inherent ambiguities—that is, ambiguities related to the fusion of an

---

* It does not matter whether such labor falls into the "purely theoretical" or "applied" categories, or what certification is required.

† "Senseless" in this context refers to the brutalizing and alienating effects of some types of work, such as industrial labor.

analytical dimension (division of labor) and a normative component (critical potential).

With the increasing importance of science and technology for the reproduction of capitalist systems, the forced separation between "idea as initiator" and "idea as product" tends to make intellectual work subject to the same "thoughtless" quality as senseless labor. This divorce fosters the notion that intellectual workers are interchangeable parts in the productive process in much the same fashion as are manual workers. A general stage of totally abstract intellectual work, however, would be difficult to implement without severely inhibiting the possibility of scientific-technical creativity, for such an abstraction depends upon eliminating the subjective element within individual ingenuity and most probably would lead to the destruction of the very talent needed for sustained economic growth. "Creativity" can, of course, exist within narrow and prescribed limits, and it can also be noncritical and nonintellectual. But such "creativity" falls outside the bounds both of a totally abstracted process of "ideas as product," and also outside the realm of intellectuality as we have defined it.

Given these conceptual clarifications, certain relationships become clear. The greater the importance of science and technology (especially after World War II), and the more apparent the crises of capitalist societies (e.g., depressions, inflation, recessions, wars, imperialism, neocolonialism, protests, mass disaffection, strikes, class struggles), the more likely it is that the critical-intellectual faculty will be made a target of sharp attacks. In an era when potential intellectuals in the *gestalt* of natural scientists, engineers, doctors, journalists, lawyers, teachers, social scientists, etc., become increasingly important to the spheres of production, distribution, reproduction of human labor, and political legitimation, a trend toward deintellectualization and the emergence (and likely triumph) of a technocratic culture become visible.

The notion of "technocratic" is somewhat more clearly defined in the social-science literature than that of "intellectual," although its meaning, too, is at times somewhat ambiguous. In this country the concept of "technocratic" is generally used in a neutral manner, mostly in the sense of "expert" tied in some fashion to merit and a measure of efficiency. In Europe it sometimes carries a derogatory connotation. In its critical aspect it is used to debunk the quasi-natural, lawlike character of the modern "postindustrial" or "technological" or "technetronic" society, in which the political choices of goals have been eliminated or reduced to the expert, "value-free" decision of one or another prescribed "choice" on the basis of a "naturally" or "systemically" given[14] or arbitrarily introduced[15] societal goal. Technocrats in the Continental definition do not reflect upon the origins and use of their knowledge and their place within society; rather, they act according to the allegedly eternal laws of science and technology—objectively. Despite their different starting points, both American and European social scientists concur in their agreement on the nonreflective character of technocrats. Thus, on both sides of the Atlantic, technocrats are the "natural" antagonists of intellectuals. For to elaborate on our definition further, intellectuality includes the human potential to reject and review given parameters, to say "no" to established epistemologies, to introduce qualitatively new ideas and to reflect on intellectual work critically within a given social context. Furthermore, intellectuality, as we understand it, is not a natural endowment nor an asset a person possesses; rather, it is the realization of a potential, usually attained through strenuous effort: it is an achievement that may quickly vanish if the effort is relaxed. But neither is it the result of purely individual efforts. On the contrary, the chance of the realization of an intellectual potential is codetermined by the societal context in which it occurs or cannot occur. It should be pointed out, however, that intellectuals in our definition are neither antiscientific nor place themselves outside the realm of science, although they do reject the rampant scientism (science as a worldview) which developed historically in response to the scientific-technical needs of modern capitalist societies (cf. neopositivism). Thus, while intellectuals transcend existing scientific paradigms, they do so by entering into the discourse in order to make an impact on its direction.

To sum up: Critical intellectuals view their approach or activity from a relativistic perspective. They are conscious of the fact that the categorical systems and methodological rules which define their

14

labor, or "intellectual game," have resulted from certain human endeavors at a given historical moment. A technocrat, by contrast, is usually a scientifically trained professional expert, who either reproduces or applies existing knowledge, expanding its scope *within* the given parameters of the existing epistemologies and a narrowly defined science, and does so without questioning the essentials of his profession, institutional setting, and society. Within the technocratic category, however, we must distinguish between those who actively propagate a technocratic ideology through a reinterpretation of societal developments in naturalistic terms (*technocratic apologists*) and the so-called practitioners who begin and end their work within the techniques alone (*technocratic specialists*).*

Despite their opposition, intellectual and technocratic activities can be and often are carried out by the same person at different times.† While ideal-typical or "pure" intellectuals and technocrats may rarely be found empirically, there has been nonetheless in the past fifty years a growing polarization between "more intellectual" and "more technocratic" persons in the United States. The reason for this split, which, we are convinced, numerically favors the technocrats, is related to the changes of Western societies from nineteenth- to twentieth-century capitalism.‡

In the end of his famous essay *The Protestant Ethic and the Spirit of Capitalism*, Max Weber as early as 1905 evoked the picture of "specialists without spirit" in a bureaucratized and mechanical capitalistic system devoid of ideas, ideals, and cultural meanings. Weber's concept of an automated capitalistic system, which "rests on mechanical foundations,"[16] seems to express his deep doubts and skepticism of the value and meaningfulness of the ongoing process of rationalization of the Western world. At first sight, the concept of a mechanical capitalism and the vision of a possible "mechanized petrification" (p. 182) of ideas and ideals developed in this essay

* This gives us three different categories of intellectuals (in addition to the common sense meaning): *critical intellectuals, technocratic apologists*, and *technocratic specialists*. We focus primarily on the first two.

† We recognize that our dichotomous typology is an abstraction from reality, in that it overemphasizes the end points of a not-yet-completed transitional period.

‡ It must be emphasized here that intellectuals in socialist countries or "societies in transition" face the same difficult conditions of realizing themselves as their counterparts in capitalist systems.

15

seem to contradict Weber's basic definition of human behavior as intentional and meaningful action.[17] However, this is not so much a logical contradiction in the work of the advocate of *verstehende Soziologie* (Interpretive Sociology) but rather a contradiction resulting from *real* changes in capitalism which he partly observed and partly anticipated, changes that tended then and still continue to remove the empirical basis of intentional actions in Weber's sense. Let us briefly consider some of these changes.

In contrast to the European societies of the nineteenth century where intellectuals, members of the new middle class and "sergeants of capital" in Marx' description, found themselves in a rather privileged position, American intellectuals have been treated less deferentially in "a society which emphasizes equality,"[18] and where eggheads are frowned upon.

Despite their relatively lower prestige, the function of American intellectuals in the establishment, integration, and stabilization of the new capitalist nation has hardly been less important than that of their European counterparts. As politicians and ideologues they helped to conceive the new nation, articulating its political principles, defending and justifying them whenever they were challenged. As missionaries and ministers they influenced the American "Protestant ethic." As teachers they helped to integrate and Americanize each wave of new immigrants. As scientists and inventors they contributed much to America's continual industrial revolution.

In the eighteenth and nineteenth centuries, the major function of the American intellectuals was ideological and apologetic, mystifying social reality rather than shedding light upon it. Still, there was intellectual and political dissent.* Influenced by a mixture of

---

* This is not the place for an in-depth review of American dissenting intellectuals. But to pique the reader's memory, let us recall some of their movements and directions. Leaving aside the Revolutionary period, the early nineteenth century saw the Transcendentalists, the Fourierists, and the Abolitionists. After the Civil War there were the theorists of the labor movement both in its trade-unionist and Marxist aspects, and the beginnings of home-grown anarchism. Scientific socialism was introduced into intellectual circles after the founding of the First International, in 1864, along with "free thought" and "free love," while other intellectuals attempted to make common cause with the populist trends of the time and forge an alliance with the "common man's" wisdom. In the eighties and nineties, anarchism came into full force, challenging the victorious economic trade-unionism of Samuel Gompers. From

Christian socialist and Marxist ideals as well as American-brand populism, critical thought, however, was more fragile and isolated, existing almost unnoticed as it grappled with its own set of historical circumstances. This is especially so when compared to the European experience, where critical thinking was under the direct influence of Marxism and an organized socialist labor movement.

During the Great Depression, the economic function of the American intellectual became clearly visible. In this regard, one has only to call to mind the many intellectuals who contributed to the avalanche of "recovery" plans and ideas funneled through the Roosevelt Administration. At the same time, the apologetic function of the intellectuals was strengthened by the very economic activities which they unfolded under the aegis of the state, for the implementation of partial and trial-and-error governmental planning not only helped to restabilize the economy but also blurred the relationship between marketplace and state power. The state's interest, under the banner of welfare capitalism, was in fact that of reorganizing society for the changed forms of capital realization which had already developed earlier in answer to the gains made during the industrial revolution. In these reequilibrating years, the country witnessed a schism in the intellectual sector. At the one end there were those who aligned themselves with the small Technocratic Party advocating an "engineering ideology,"[19] and at the other, the organized coalition of labor and left intellectuals. In other words, when the American system became more dependent on the loyal cooperation of its intellectuals, *and* the system, undergoing its first major industrial-economic crisis, found itself challenged by an apparently viable alternative economic system and political ideology (the successful Bolshevik Revolution), the first definite signs of a polarization among "intellectuals" between radical dissenters and conservative technocrats became clearly apparent.

the turn of the century to World War I, the so-called progressive era housed various brands of socialists, muckrakers, and the Harlem Renaissance intellectuals.

During the nineteen-thirties, the Left was split between the two Marxist parties, Communists and Socialists and other minor spin-offs, while radical liberals gave their full support to social reform. The energies of many intellectuals during and after World War II were consumed first by the struggle against fascism and then by the protection of American democracy against communism. The sixties, an era with which we are more familiar, saw the formation of the New Left, a surge of Neo-Marxist and antiauthoritarian modes of thought as well as the re-emergence of a liberation movement among black intellectuals.

After World War II, two other trends in American society played a significant role: the enormous expansion of the higher-education system (primarily a result of an explosion of, and uneven development in, both supply and demand),[20] and the growing importance of the state as an employer of professionally trained people.

In the sixties, with science and technology already recognized as a major source of economic growth and with intellectuals "approaching the position of being most important in American society,"[21] and with the university itself being redefined as a "public-service" institution, it is no surprise that Nettl (among others) notes the fact that in "many countries, especially in the United States, universities have today become loci of institutionalized dissent" (p. 87).

One can infer from these historical examples, then, that the greater the strategic and systemic importance of intellectuals, the more they acquire conflict potential, becoming at one and the same time a potential source of radical social change *and* the target of massive attempts at cooptation, persuasion, and oppression.[22]

Considering now the three major changes of American society as they bear on the position of intellectuals, we suggest the following: the greater number of intellectuals contributes to their further declassification. Their systemic importance subjects those employed in industry, private business, and educational institutions to the exploitation, alienation, frustration, and stress hitherto associated with industrial labor (i.e., they take on classlike characteristics). As more become state employees, finally, they are no longer directly linked to capitalist interests nor affected by the crudent forms of capitalist work conditions; instead, they experience the relative deprivation of the public sector.

Marginal Groups

> The third category of the relative overpopulation, the stagnant, is part of the active army of workers with irregular employment. It thus offers capital an inexhaustible reservoir of a disposable labor force. Its standard of living sinks below the average normal standard of the working class, and it is this that makes it the broad base of special exploitation mechanisms of capi-

18

tal....Aside from vagabonds, criminals, prostitutes, in short, the lumpenproletariat, this class consists of three categories: First, employables ... secondly, orphans and children of paupers ... thirdly, the degenerated, the racked, the unemployables....The greater the societal wealth, the functioning capital, the scope and energy of its growth, hence also the absolute size of the proletariat and the productivity of its labor, the larger the industrial reserve army....The relative size of the industrial reserve army increases with the potency of wealth....Thus the accumulation of wealth, on the one hand, is simultaneous with the accumulation of misery, torture (by labor), slavery, igno-rance, brutalization, and moral desolation, on the other.

Karl Marx, *Das Kapital*[23]

Marx's concept of a "disposable labor force" finds a stunning referent in the conditions of slum life in the United States, including the situation of the old and disabled, of the unemployed and unemployables. In current parlance they are called the "marginals." Marx's description of their "miserableness," cutting through his nineteenth-century prose, has come to pass. The reality of American society is one in which tremendous accumulation and concentration of wealth coexists with relative poverty and economic exploitation, exacerbated by a system of ethnic stratification and racism which he could not visualize.

In the late fifties and sixties, some racial and ethnic groups organized themselves and demanded access to the wealth of the system. The movement of American blacks became the prototype of protest carried by marginal groups both in its organized (civil-rights movement, Black Panther Party) and disorganized (cf. riots, delinquency) forms. Their concentration in the big cities, their apparent potential for destructive violence on a nationwide scale (e.g., the 1968 riots after the murder of Martin Luther King, Jr.), as well as the recent formation of other protest-prone marginal groups (e.g., those based on sex and age) led some social scientists to conclude that the structural source of radical change lay in the "peripheral zones" of society. While they employ "periphery" and "marginality status" to mean exclusion from the productive sector, the two terms stem from separate levels of understanding about the interconnectedness of class and ethnic status in the stratified American system. "Periphery" relates to the location of a group in

19

function of its distance from the strategic core of roundabout production (e.g., capital goods are at the center relative to commodity and service goods). In this sense, periphery is related to a class structure based on production, but in the American case is in fact equated with the concept of "underclass" or the *Lumpen*. The "peripheral zone" thus becomes synonymous with poverty, whether connected with the unemployables, underemployed, or unemployed.

"Marginality" is related to the location of persons as regards their "status" in a dominant-subdominant power scale (or degrees of deprivation). In the American case, marginality is linked to ascribed characteristics—race and ethnicity, which have long been associated with subdominant-powerless status. Race, ethnicity, poverty, powerlessness—i.e., class by being "nonclass" and ascribed status by "historical association"—mesh together to describe the potential agencies of societal disruption for peripheral-zone theorists. The entrance of student protest and women's liberation, generally white and middle-class, into the movement against the *status quo* posed problems for this descriptive analysis. Although by virtue of age and sex they fell into the category of ascribed-status groups, their obvious "class" positions contradicted the poverty link to class analysis postulated by peripheral theory. By encompassing the middle-class student because of his extended though temporary "marginality status," and the white middle-class woman because of her subordinate role, these interpreters claim that their drive for mobilization and their apparent politicization stems solely from their "marginality status."

Peripheral theory has provided a descriptive framework for dealing with the recent societal tensions and has correctly redrawn attention to the continued historical significance of ascribed status groups in the U.S. But the theory demands further clarification with respect to the locus of political dissent, for ascribed marginality—if dissociated from class and taken as the sole basis of organization—is likely to lead to individualistic and nonpolitical forms of protest. In order to arrive at an adequate evaluation of the radical potential of the current protest phenomena, we will have carefully to discern their structural underpinnings, whether they be class, marginality status, or a combination of both. While we do not believe that it is possible to construct a strictly causal relationship between objective situation and forms of action, we do suggest that the tempo and direction of political learning processes leading people to act upon their condition are mediated with the objectively existing situations and the images of reality connected with them.

Protest, Class, and Marginality Groups

Recalling our thesis about the essential interconnectedness of student and racial or ethnic protest, we have now reached a point where the results of our separate conceptual explorations of each of these phenomena can be put into perspective. We suggest that the organization and dynamics of the political learning processes of these groups cannot be understood unless one takes into account the historical circumstances which characterize the evolving class arrangements, intellectual horizons, and cultural traditions of these two groups. In contrast to an abstract idealization of the working class and its revolutionary potential, or the glorification of intellectuals as the only carriers of critical dissent in modern societies, we hold that the manifestations of protest in the student-intellectual sector and in the periphery of the system during the sixties and seventies signal the beginning of a practical application of the critical potential to the immediate experiences of these groups as they relate to the society at large.

What is structurally new in the postwar decades is the growing consciousness and at times planned efforts on the part of elite groups to reorganize education and the scientific process to bring it more directly in line with the changed nature of techniques and scientific methodology for capital formation.

For students in the sixties this reorganization, which had already taken on full-blown proportions, meant that their particular place in the university made them (not occurring to all simultaneously, however) able to make out their new "subjugated importance." What in fact had happened—and what lay at the core of their discontent—was their growing recognition that their future scholarship and scientific ingenuity were no longer tenuously

21

mediated with the capitalist work process but were becoming directly affected.

Marginals—for the summary of our argument let us stick with the black population—have always been subjugated. In this particular context we refer to the fact that they have been "on call," serving within the work force only when specific productive needs had to be filled. Their history is peppered with their cries against this direct type of exploitation with changed tunes, depending on their state of "in-ness" or "out-ness." They thus have stored in their "memory-banks" the experience of being "out" when "in" and vice-versa. As a result of World War II, more individual blacks were integrated into the work force on a more permanent basis, but the static condition of the black masses became more obvious, because as production was evolving into a more capital-intensive process, full integration of blacks turned out to be an illusion. In the process, more blacks started to see the relationship between class and race.

As black protest and consciousness and student dissent encountered each other, the learning process between the two groups became a two-way street and provided the possibility for a real radical questioning of the system as a whole. (Radicalization in this context refers to the fact that members of each group learned to act upon their own interests and at the same time became aware of their mutual class positions.) It is in the structural condition of marginality status and class and the contours of this new political constellation, however fragile, that we see a radical potential to challenge inequality in the United States.

PART
II
AN ANATOMY OF SOCIAL SCIENCE EXPLANATIONS FOR STUDENT PROTEST

2
THE SETTING
AND SOME
METHODOLOGICAL
CONSIDERATIONS

I

In 1960, four black student freshmen at the North Carolina Agricultural and Technical College sat down at a for "Whites Only" F. W. Woolworth lunch counter in Greensboro, North Carolina, and waited for service. They never got their lunch. Instead, they launched an avalanche directed against Southern institutions and the Southern legal *status quo*. Disparate acts at first, sit-ins soon coalesced to form the new civil-rights movement: a loose coalition of blacks and whites, Northerners and Southerns, students and nonstudents.[1] Although the movement had at its center only a small hard core of adherents, it received massive national support and participation in its Mississippi voter registration drive (Corfo Summer, 1964) and in the 1965 march from Selma to Montgomery, Alabama. Organizationally, the coalition was made up of CORE (Congress for Racial Equality, founded in 1943 in Chicago), SCLC (Southern Christian Leadership Conference, founded in 1957 in Atlanta), and SNCC (Student Nonviolent Coordinating Committee, founded in 1960 in Raleigh—the only actual student organization), and a handful of unaffiliated individuals. Its strategy during the early sixties was "direct action," and its style, following the lead of the Reverend Martin Luther King, Jr., was nonviolent. Both strategy and style, however, were short-lived.

The failure of the reformist, integrationist civil-rights movement to work rapid and effective change in the conditions under which the black masses lived was made relentlessly clear by the spontaneous rash of urban riots that swept the country, starting with Watts in 1965. The negative experiences of both black and white student organizations (SDS—Students for a Democratic Society, founded at the University of Michigan in 1960—and SNCC) in their attempts to go to the "people" and organize an interracial class movement seemed to persuade the "freedom now" generation of the inefficacy of liberal strategies and styles. As a result, the direction of the movement changed, especially in its student sector, to a search for more radical and militant alternatives.

By the mid-sixties, a distinct student movement had emerged, but now black and white interests were no longer explicitly joined. The Free Speech Movement's rally in front of Sproul Hall at the University of California at Berkeley in 1964 had spectacularly demonstrated that confrontationist methods (learned during the nonviolent civil-rights campaigns in the South) could be effectively used in the fight against the bureaucratic structure of the university. SDS followed the FSM's lead, and in 1965 made the university campuses its power base from which to launch its attempts to change American society. With the escalation of the Vietnam war in 1965, antiwar sentiment joined with student protest against the new productive function of the multiversity, its complicity with the military-industrial complex, and its "irrelevant" curricula and "mechanical" education.

For about four years following the Berkeley affair, white student protest dominated the national college scene with escalating confrontations and increasing violence. Clashes between administration and students at Columbia University on the East Coast and San Francisco State College on the West Coast in 1968 signaled a shift in the actors and a change in priorities. The fall and spring terms of 1968 and 1969 saw black student protest and black issues taking the lead in terms of frequency and intensity of campus-based protest.[2] In large measure this shift was due to the search for radical departures from the civil-rights movement. Many blacks, particularly students and intellectuals, had become convinced that an evolving "black identity" was a perequisite for changing the black condition. After a quasi-moratorium of three years, black students started to issue demands for increased racial quotas in the educational system and an ideological change of the curriculum. However, "racism" in all its facets and manifestations remained their concern. With this revitalized thrust, and perhaps because the "symbol" of American imperialism, President Johnson, had bowed out and withdrawn his name from the presidential race of 1968, white students became followers in the movement of blacks against institutional racism.

But the issues of war, racism, and official violence were to become shockingly linked again in the murders of black students at Jackson State College and white students at Kent State University. Both black and white students called for a nationwide strike in April, 1970. "Cambodian Spring" saw college students spearheading the revulsion of the nation against physical and psychological violence both at home and abroad. To stem the tide of near rebellion, university administrators and federal authorities made "reasoned" concessions: President·Nixon "limited" his Cambodian invasion; commissions of inquiry into student unrest and national violence were set up; quota representation (later to become known as "affirmative action") became official experimental guidelines; and talk of educational reform was heard in the halls of academe.

After that climactic and explosive spring, the struggle to end the war shifted to the Congress and to the political parties, while the fight against racism was diverted to include the implementation of equal representation of *all* minority and marginal groups. Following *Realpolitik*, a political settlement brought the withdrawal of American troops from Vietnam, although economic and strategic weapons are still doing battle. The fact that there has been little or no visible political activity on the campuses in recent months has led to the suggestion in some quarters that campus apathy is but another example of adolescent extremism, or even more self-seeking,

27

that the termination of the draft and the subsequent removal of immediate personal danger is responsible for the apathy. Explanatory speculation also vaccilates between self-satisfaction—the American people, as is their wont, have seen the merit of student and black grievances, and woven them into the laws of the land—and fear—students have withdrawn from politics because of political oppression or, more dangerously, have withdrawn their consent (however silent) to be governed. For a while, during the election campaigns of 1972, observers thought that campus apathy reflected a shift from frontal attack to infiltration of the Democratic party in an attempt by young people to work within the system for the changes they sought. But, for the pragmatic speculator, the change has been laid at the door of economic uncertainty: students have returned to the business of worrying about good grades to get good jobs.

II

Introduction to the Ideologiekritik of Explanations for Student Protest

The American public was at first startled and confused by the sudden outbreak of student unrest among apparently well-to-do white students attending the nation's most prestigious colleges. The immediate rationalizations for their behavior ranged from scoffs at the "panty-raid" syndrome to petulance, because the young did not appreciate the favored position and good fortune that was theirs. As student rebellion spread and their targets came dangerously close to sacred and revered American homilies, however, Americans sat up and took another look. As tactics affronted good taste and the general sense of decorum, the nation knew that an ill wind was sweeping the country. The uneasiness became even more pervasive when student rebellion merged with the growing militancy and rebellion of the blacks and urban poor. And as could be expected, the cumulative bombardment led to the public's rallying around one or another proffered common-sense explanation, whether it came from the press, the government, the literati, or the barroom.

28

Depending on such factors as social class, political affiliation, degree of involvement, self-image,[3] student as well as black protest was perceived as "legitimate social protest," "rebellion," "revolution," or "criminal acts." The actions were alternately attributed to a "communist conspiracy of subversive outside agitators," "the too-liberal climate on college campuses," "moral decadence," or "socioeconomic deprivation." Most explanations came complete with solutions: concentration camps, police on campus, "America, love it or leave it!," more discipline in the family and college, or, in more conciliatory tones, a call for increased funds for education, housing, and welfare for the "deserving" poor.

Social scientists were also surprised by the protest movement of the sixties. As late as 1961, three years before Berkeley and one year after the founding of SNCC and SDS, Talcott Parsons described American students as being especially well integrated into society.[4] Neither his nor other theoretical frameworks elaborated in the post–World War II period had apparently allowed for the identification of those tendencies in the educational system which might have enabled them to suspect, let alone predict, the possibility of widespread disaffection and protest among students (or blacks, for that matter) in the sixties. But as the record will show, the social scientists were not lacking in hard data, for the student population was widely studied during that period.[5] The purely descriptive categories prescribed by these models, however, seemed to bind them to the immediately recognizable reality—the "cool and uncommitted," politically apathetic students of the fifties.

Post factum, protest events have been described, analyzed, surveyed, data-banked, compared, and ideologically debated by a vast army of scholars, participant observers, hard-data analysts, and armchair philosophers. The product of this voluminous output is a series of unconnected hypotheses drawn from various currently held theoretical and methodological approaches. The result is even more confounding because many empirical studies have designed *ad hoc* hypotheses to fit a particular case of protest. Although almost all of the social-science disciplines have contributed their points of view to the description and explanation of student unrest, a theoretical discussion between them has only recently begun.[6] In the following

29

sections, we critically review the principal social-scientific explanations of left student protest and marginal groups as they impinge on the movement in the hope that this will help to further the discussion. At times we will also draw on the body of literature produced by the protesters themselves, since New Left and black intellectuals have also been concerned with political-programmatic discussions of goals, strategies, and tactics as well as with a critical evaluation of their actions and learning processes. The literature of these groups delineate this intensive political reflection. The concept of marginality status is explored under economic explanations, Chapter Five. In that section, peripheral theory is not only broadly outlined, but its particular application to student and black protest critically assessed. Marginality status as an important rallying point for past or potential revolt is an important dimension in Chapters Nine and Ten.

Causal and functional *explanations* of student unrest, whether explicitly or implicitly stated, are the material of our review.[7] Since definition and description are necessary parts of every scientific explanation, both will be considered in the analysis.[8] In addition, we will examine the various *conceptions* of student protest referring to their nature as well as to their social meaning for the larger society.

The political, economic, social, and educational consequences which are either directly suggested or can be extrapolated are yet another aspect. We are specifically interested in whether and to what extent such theories lend themselves to being legitimations—or ideologies in the classical sense*—of the *status quo*. Our procedure thus follows the methodology of *Ideologiekritik* which is widely employed by critical West German social scientists.†

By means of *Ideologiekritik* we will within the theories about student protest attempt to separate those elements (i.e., categories,

* We refer here to the Marxian conception of ideology. For Marx, scientific theories, ideas, legal systems, philosophy, religion, and other manifestations of the "superstructure" were ideological if they were based on *abstract* speculation *and* as such served the interests of the ruling class. Marx proved that in his time abstract philosophy (such as Hegel's idealism) and abstract science (such as bourgeois economics) provided the bourgeoisie with legitimations of their political-economic interests.

† This approach was made famous by members of the Frankfurt School of Sociology: Theodor W. Adorno, Max Horkheimer, Herbert Marcuse, and among the younger generation, particularly by Jürgen Habermas.

descriptions) which adequately, if unwittingly, depict and illustrate the real phenomena from those *elements* which veil or distort the actual nature of the social processsses in question. To arrive at the first, the theories must be analyzed in the context of the development of the concrete society of which they are a part, while the second are discerned by contrasting the surface appearances with the "inner" development of society.* In the following sections the social-scientific theories of student protest will thus be evaluated according to the extent to which they reveal the hidden social factors and processes that determine the changes of American society and affect the lives of its citizens. This criterion implies that theories which turn out to be mere reflections of the prevailing mood, and thus incapable of anticipating "sudden" developments, are ideological, even though they may claim to be methodologically "objective" and "value-free."

In order to avoid a righteous tinge or prevent an out-of-hand rejection of a theory *in toto*,† *Ideologiekritik* must be sufficiently rooted in a substantive theory (i.e., filled with content) of society. That is, a critical assessment of social-science theories of protest must take account of the essential unity of the scientific and the actual historical process. Ideological elements of consciousness, belief, ideas, theories, etc, can only be discerned if the movements of the larger society are comprehended. Only then can one judge the extent to which theories camouflage and distort social reality in order to arrest it. *Ideologiekritik* as a methodology thus reiterates the epistemological dilemma which is constitutive for the social sciences

---

* The "inner" structure of society refers to its essence and "real" movements, in contrast to those changes that appear on its surface. Hegel was the first to develop and apply his dialectical method in order to comprehend the essential unity and the inner coherence of different individual phenomena. Marx changed Hegel's idealistic approach into a dialectical materialist method. Cf. Karl Marx, *Das Kapital*, I, *MEW*, XXIII (Berlin: Dietz Verlag, 1972), 27 f.

† The simplistic characterization of a whole theory as "ideological" or "bourgeois," which is often employed by orthodox Marxists, occasionally finds its correlate in an equally simplistic acceptance of the results of a "bourgeois" science *in toto*, on the basis of which "critical theory" proceeds. The latter method is characteristic of some works of the Frankfurt School of Sociology. See e.g., Marcuse's introduction to his *One-Dimensional Man*, especially p. XVII. For the programmatic concept of "critical theory" and its relation to bourgeois disciplines, see Max Horkheimer, "Traditionelle und kritische Theorie," *Zeitschrift für Sozialforschung*, VI, No. 7 (Paris, 1937), 245 ff.

as a whole: it requires a theory of society which on its part is codetermined by concrete societal tendencies. There is yet another problem. Following the dialectical approach, *Ideologiekritik* takes cognizance of the essentially processual character of social reality. That is, social interpretations, be they popular ideas, beliefs, or social-scientific theories, turn into ideological legitimations if they negate the historical limitedness of the *status quo* by denying the possibilities of historical alternatives. Historical alternatives, however, cannot be simply projected as opposites of the existing situation. Rather, they exist within the given cultural and societal matrix as viable visions of transcending conditions. They are brought about by people's choices to act upon objectively given circumstances. An *Ideologiekritik* directed at an ongoing process operates within a relatively open historical horizon and, because it can neither fully predict human action nor fully identify the direction of change without denying the element of choice, runs the risk of misjudging the importance and ideological character of certain trends.

Depending on the structure and the historically concrete situation of a given society, ideologies may be pervasive and take on the form of a seemingly "free" consensus about the societal order or be primarily carried and promoted by the class most interested in the perpetuation of the *status quo*. In either case, however, ideologies contain elements within themselves which often turn their major function, the consolidation of an existing state of society, into its very opposite. The American Dream "that the free society and the good society could be realized together in America"[9] is just one example of such an ideology based on a "free consensus." The vision and ideal of the American society expressed in the American Dream has served the function of safeguarding this country against political-ideological challenges and class struggle. It was both a revolutionary national principle of the American bourgeoisie, for whom liberty was identical with economic freedom, and a liberal social utopia whose realization was conceived as attainable within the given capitalist framework and declared the goal of the further development of American society. Inasmuch as the American Dream projects the vision of a just society for all Americans, it has often provided American social critics with a standard against which they could measure the concrete reality of their society and on the basis of which demands for broadening access for previously excluded groups have repeatedly been articulated. The utopian elements of the American Dream have often initiated reform processes, but they never threatened the existing order as long as the system was ready and able to respond successfully to liberal critique and reformist demands. Once the system loses this capability, however, the dialectic of reform and revolution sets in: reformist critics (e.g., the adherents of the civil rights movement), realizing that their demands (e.g., racial integration) cannot be met under the prevailing economic conditions, turn radical (cf. SNCC, Black Panther Party) and start to challenge the limits of the system itself.

To sum up: *Ideologiekritik* as a methodology of the social sciences must take into account the interplay of political-economic trends and human *praxis*. Being part of societal totality, its results may possibly help to initiate and influence the direction of political actions.

The procedural problem of seeing the society in the round and of seeing the theories about the protest movements as part of the whole and getting it down on paper, necessarily implies a certain awkwardness. In the following pages, theories about protest are considered typologically, by psychological, political, economic, and cultural criteria.* It must nevertheless be kept in mind that our critique will be fully carried through only after it has been complemented by a sketch of the historical development of American society (Chapter Nine).

---

* We have constructed this typology in order to survey the social-science literature on student protest so that its *locus* in the different realms of society may be indicated. Our procedure departs from Weber's arbitrary selection of characteristics molded into his ideal types in that our categorical structuring of the literature reflects the actual fabric of the protest scene and its social-scientific conceptualizations.

3

THE PSYCHOLOGICAL MODEL

The psychological explanation locates the roots of student protest in the extraordinary personality traits of a relatively small number of activist students who are considered exceptions, unlike the normal, predominantly apathetic and "privatistic" student majority. The methods of psychological exploration used differ widely, ranging from psychoanalysis to superficial interview techniques. The value judgments implied in or attached to these explanations seem also to represent a wide variety of positions, ranging from quick condemnation to supportive sympathy. One characteristic, however, is common to almost every psychological explanation: a tendency to explain away the subjects of the actions, the students. They pigeonhole them either (1) *social-psychologically* (protest is the product of an overpermissive socialization resulting in spoiled, intolerant, irresponsible adolescents with infantile responses);[1] (2) *sociologically* (activists come from professional, upper-middle-class, liberal families and are outstanding students with strong academic commitments and a "basic allegiance to creedal American ideals");[2] (3) *psychiatrically* (protest is the result of traumatic early childhood experiences and rebellion against parents);[3] (4) *situationally* (student protest is a pattern of adjustment to the "depersonalized," "dehumanized" college education of today[4] or to the status incon-

35

sistencies students encounter in contemporary American society);[5] and finally, (5) *generationally* (student protest is an outgrowth of adolescence, a transitory phase whose difficulties result from changes in society).[6]

These explanations not only negate the students as subjects of the protest, but in their emphasis on mental, subjective, or atypical factors they are also inherently ahistorical and overlook the rootedness of the protest movement in a set of social circumstances. It can be assumed, for example, that there have always been maladjusted, frustrated, outstanding, or supercritical students, but the question remains why these students (if indeed they do fit these descriptions) are launching such strong protest *today*. Or, to pose another question: Is it only a small outstanding elite or a small number of psychologically maladjusted students who are currently engaged in protest? How do we then "explain" the 1969–70 demonstrations at "average" colleges, including all-girl, denominational, rural as well as professional schools, and which attracted students from all social classes? Correlation analyses may point out that student protest occurs more often at certain urban and elite liberal-arts institutions, but they do not explain why and how protest activities developed in practically all sectors of the educational system (including high schools). The fact that some students are more active and that some institutions encounter more protest has attracted the interest of social scientists to such a degree that they have forgone the explanation of student protest as a whole and its development over time. (The same has happened to explanations of black and ghetto riots). The analyses which emphasize the atypical nature of a specific group of students are also limited in their explanatory power in that they hypostatize a particular aspect or a particular stage of the student movement as a whole.[7] They do not consider or account for individual and collective learning processes among the activist nucleus or the rank-and-file members. Very few of the authors offering a psychological or social-psychological explanation of student protest have reached Flacks' conclusion that "a full understanding of the dynamics of the movement requires a 'collective behavior' perspective" and that the characteristics of the movement "cannot be understood solely as

consequences of the structural and personality variables. . ."[8]
Finally, it appears that whatever the points of departure of these
authors, the standard to which they compare their findings and
prescriptions is a model of a pluralist democratic society.*

Student Protesters and Their Parents

Viewing the student activists in relation to their parents, the
following is being suggested in the literature: student revolutionaries are products of an overpermissive socialization. Often the result
is deplored (by the observer) and the parents are blamed for their
Spock-inspired child-rearing practices. This formulation is heavily
value-laden, as the term "*over*permissive" clearly indicates, and its
proponents usually call for more discipline and responsibility-
oriented family situations and schooling. In this respect they show a
striking resemblance to Talcott Parsons' system-maintenance
postulate.†

The overpermissiveness hypothesis differs from the following,
more widely held position only in its derogatory character.
According to Keniston, Flacks, and others, student activists tend to
come from well-educated, well-to-do, liberal families who generally
support the political cause of their children and encourage them to
be critical and independent, to seek self-realization and develop
their creativity.

Political student activists, observe Keniston and others who hold
this view, do not protest for their own personal interest but identify
with the economically oppressed all over the world. Since their
protest does not grow out of their own socioeconomic conditions, the
argument runs, students themselves cannot be so easily coopted by a
system which tends to resolve its conflicts by economic rewards. At
the same time, however, the politically involved as opposed to
"culturally alienated" students, can still be explained—and
contained—within the American tradition. They are "the vanguard
of a new wave of extension of universalism in American society,"
and their demands "reflect . . . one of the continuing trends in

* See pp. 50 ff.
† See pp. 40 ff. below.

American social change."[9] "Culturally alienated" students, on the other hand, who come from the same select family background, question the very principles of capitalist societies: achievement and competition, material rewards and alienated labor, bureaucratization and the lack of aesthetic and expressive values. Taking wealth and a high technological standard for granted, these students, so the argument continues, challenge the traditional ethics of capitalism because they experience frustrations in the spiritual, aesthetic, and personal realms which are being suppressed by the mechanisms and structure of a capitalistic society.*

How will the protest of the advantaged youth develop? The various scholars differ in their predictions, depending on their own political positions: while Habermas sees a chance that this protest, which is so difficult to coopt, may in the long run debunk the legitimations of late capitalist systems, Peter Berger [10] suggests that the large bureaucracies will compromise with the youth culture and thereby incorporate it. Or, according to a later statement of his,[11] the alienated advantaged youth will be replaced in high positions by the status-oriented blue-collar youth who are still "making it" in the system. Keniston foresees continued protest as long as minorities are excluded from the mainstream of the American system and technological society remains void of humanitarian and expressive values.

The argument that student protesters are a select group without any traumatic personal experiences is challenged by some psychoanalysts. On the basis of psychoanalytic in-depth interviews, Hendin for example suggests that student revolutionaries tend to have been "emotionally abandoned" by their parents. "These young radicals have suffered in families which more than provided for their material needs but which ignored and frustrated their personal needs and continue to be blind to them as people."[12] Student protest is thus conceived as being the product of an unresolved conflict *within* the family. Political activities and life with fellow revolutionaries serve as substitute satisfactions of personal needs. (This same argument was used in the early sixties to explain

* It should be noted here that the distinction between "activist" and "culturally alienated" students applies only to the American scene.

the rash of youthful marriages.) Student protest, according to this hypothesis, is rooted in the emotional deprivation of economically overprivileged children by their own parents, and not, as Keniston and others suggest, in the materialism of society outside the family.

Student Protest and the University

Student protest in relation to the educational institutions is explained as a failure to adjust to the depersonalized bureaucratic multiversity. These students, the prognosis runs, are alienated in the anonymous megastructures of the modern universities and need counseling and psychiatric help as well as guidance to regain "mental health" and guarantee their academic performance. This approach defines student protest as one type of adjustment to an existing system in utter disregard of the *content* of the students' demands.

Another situational explanation of student protest is offered on the basis of the seemingly contradictory role definition of students in American society. Kaplan, for example, points out the discrepancies that exist between a student's relatively high prestige outside the university on the basis of his future career and his oppression within the university, where he finds himself at the bottom of the status ladder. Another ambivalence results from the fact that the student is considered an adult as far as his academic performance and military service are concerned (in the case of males), and not yet an adult in his sexual life and political interests. Further insecurity is generated by the fear of academic failure as well as the fact that many students have not yet developed a definite occupational goal. According to this approach, student unrest has its basis in these status discrepancies and the resulting anxieties and aggressions, all of which are considered transitory phenomena that need personal adjustment and not political initiatives on part of the students. Yet, despite this "diagnosis" students for some unexplained reason become politically motivated.

Student Protest and Adolescence

One widely accepted proposition holds that student unrest is the

39

manifestation of a generational conflict. More precisely, it is seen as resulting from the developmental problems and severe identity crises connected with the stage of adolescence, a transitory phase "which most authors regard as a period of generalized rebellion in American society."[13]

The authors who attempt to explain overt student protest within this framework base their studies on either one of two theoretical approaches, both of which stress elements of latent conflicts in the secondary socialization process, conflicts which will eventually develop into manifest protest. The first approach is psychoanalytical (or perhaps, better, psychohistorical) and was developed by Erik H. Erikson.[14] The second is the structural-functional approach as developed by S. N. Eisenstadt[15] and Talcott Parsons.[16]

Erikson argues that adolescents undergo a major identity crisis and have many personal conflicts while struggling for adulthood and forming a "mature psychosocial identity" (p. 231). Therefore, most cultures grant their young a so-called "psychosocial moratorium"—a period during which they can try out various sets of roles which will eventually become the framework for their new self-definition. According to this theory, the adult identity results from a synthesis of rebellion against and identification with specific characteristics, parental values, and the established patterns of the social environment. Identity formation in this sense implies the search for social continuity in terms of a development that would connect elements of the past with the present and the future on the individual as well as the group level. Erikson points out repeatedly that identity formation is dependent on two kinds of time: "a *developmental* stage in the life of the individual, and a *period* in history" (p. 242). The intensity of individual rebellion depends on whether the individual finds a possibility of developing satisfactory and acceptable identity within the framework of the traditional value patterns and the anticipated future. In times of rapid social change, when traditional values and group norms are being questioned, adolescents will find it more difficult to form a psychosocial identity. In this instance, Erikson argues, there is "a complementarity of life-history and history," and adolescent rebellion against specific norms becomes identical with a collective search for a new group identity. Then "the crisis of youth is also the crisis of a generation and the ideological soundness of its society" (p. 242). Erikson's line of reasoning obviously excepts him from the criticisms concerning the generally ahistorical nature of the usual psychological approach.

Erikson has repeatedly demonstrated the usefulness of this theoretical model in the explanation and conceptualization of different historical cases of individual and group identity formation, as for example, in his *Young Man Luther*[17] and his essays on Negro identity. But the limitations of this approach became obvious in the hands of his followers when they used it alternately to describe and explain conservative as well as progressive rebellion.[18] It seems, therefore, that, in order to find explanations for specific rebellions, protest movements, and revolutions, Erikson's psychohistorical categories must be complemented by a socioeconomic analysis of the society in which the young rebels grow up. The limitations and implications of this approach become even more evident in the studies of the sit-in movement in the American South and black student protest conducted by Fishman and Solomon.[19] Because of the "unique susceptibility and responsiveness of youth to would-be social change",[20] they sought to identify the political, ideological, and social factors that influenced the actions of the young protesters. Their analysis of U.S. society, however, is limited to isolated moments (e.g. the Supreme Court decision on school desegregation) and is carried out on the purely subjective level, reconstructing the reality perceived and remembered by their respondents. History becomes a series of anecdotes.

In the weakness of their interpretation of student unrest as typical of adolescent behavior lies the possibility that they can be (and are) sympathetic to the protest of the young students, whose actions for them have a quasi-natural basis in their age category, but they cannot explain the protest of young (or older) adults without seeing their actions as the pathological product of a prolonged adolescence.[21]

The political position of the two investigators is clearly set forth in their discussion of their research interests:

> We should be particularly concerned with the kind of

41

socialization process and conditions which gear youth to social action within the framework of an open democratic society, on the one hand, and that which predisposes or forces youth into an extremist position, leading to violent revolution or totalitarianism, quite opposite from the interests and ideals of our own society, on the other.[22]

To the question they pose to themselves, "How can an open democratic society provide youth with the models and outlets for rebellion and assertion which youth needs, without grave risk to the stability of the society?" they answer—the Peace Corps, career training programs or "pro-social activities" like the nonviolent civil-rights movement. Their concern is for the needs and mental health of the adolescents, a concern proper for psychiatrists. Their goal is obviously not the critical analysis of a society which they have defined as "an open democratic" system—a definition and acceptance of values (in addition to a muddling of the concepts of "revolution" and "totalitarianism") radically questioned and challenged by the very youth for whom Solomon and Fishman show such concern but whom they would like to manipulate. They would have protesters learn to share the basic values of the system and not present a "grave risk to the stability of the society."[23]

We now turn to the systematic theory of generations which S. N. Eisenstadt has developed within the theoretical framework of structural functionalism. He suggests that youth cultures and movements develop in institutionally differentiated societies in which the family can no longer provide the role models that individuals must learn in order to manipulate their milieu. In societies with a high degree of economic and social division of labor, individuals, he argues, must develop adult role dispositions outside the family, that is, primarily in contact with peer groups, in schools, universities, and other societal institutions. In this situation the young person encounters a value conflict between the most important agents of socialization, the family, stressing solidarity, expressivity and particularism, on the one hand, and schools and universities, emphasizing competition, achievement orientation, and universalism, on the other. These latter institutions become the targets of aggression on part of the adolescents, because they transmit the "adult" values. According to this theory then, student rebellion is the result of adjustment problems caused by structural discontinuities of the basic values and behavior patterns in the family, school, and university. While Eisenstadt acknowledges the existence of conflict elements in the secondary socialization process, he seems to suggest that a certain price must be paid for the successful integration of the young into the complex world of modern society. His theory, however, contains no clues as to why the stress situation and latent conflicts associated with adolescence should lead to *politically* motivated protest among the youth. On the basis of this theory and Eisenstadt's analysis, it is safe to say that young people are more likely to protest in times of rapid social change.[24] But, how does one formulate any hypothesis concerning the immediate cause, intensity, or extent of student protest? Furthermore, the question whether overt protests may be caused by repressive elements contained in the socializing institutions is not discussed, nor for that matter are alternative routes to so-called "modern" societies.

Lewis Feuer used this theory of generation primarily to polemicize against the rebelling students at Berkeley,[25] and Paul Seabury in order to "explain" the rebellion of assistants against professors at the Free University of Berlin.[26] We will by-pass the many empirical studies based on this model or the simplifications thereof. Talcott Parsons' most recent thesis, on the other hand, calls for further discussion. As we have mentioned earlier, Parsons had posited in 1961 that the youth of a predominantly middle-class industrialized society was not likely to engage in significant social or generational conflict.[27] This, he held, was because the young had been adequately socialized into accepting the modern (i.e., occupational) values of the older generation, which, in turn, minimized the possible disjunction between the values of the two generations.

Writing in 1970,[28] however, Parsons (together with Gerald Platt) implicitly recognizes that the current student population is *not* well integrated into the system. He consequently views them as immature persons who have not yet reached adulthood, belonging to a subculture geared to the values of "peer solidarity, equality, and functional diffuseness" (p. 12). Adults, on the other hand, are those who have internalized the core societal values of "differential

43

achievement" and have accepted the "functionally necessary authority" (p. 11). The above "reality," together with the prerequisite importance of mass higher education for effective collective participation in modern society, suggests for him that a new phase in the socialization process—studentry—must be isolated and understood. Since the primary characteristic of this phase is diffuse peer solidarity, which is contrary to society's needs, it must somehow be repressed in order "for the components of adult personality to develop" (p. 28).

Since the student, from this perspective, is seen as immature, the university must assume the role of a socializing agent under the broad directive of readying him "in the interest of the value-based collective system" (p. 11). Naturally, if the university is the protector of acceptable behavior, the student cannot and should not be allowed to participate in any university decisions concerning its structure or curriculum. This leads to the conclusion that Parsons and those who share his position apparently justify and hold as "good" the present organization and power structure of the university.

Both Eisenstadt's and Parsons' analysis and argumentation are presented within the framework of a normative-empirical theory which is politically conservative in its consequences. The normatively introduced frame of reference is the existing industrial society, to which both universities and students must adapt. Within this way of thinking, a university which would define the critical analysis of society as one of its goals is not conceivable; neither is a student-faculty relationship of the two groups as partners within the academic community; neither is any consideration given to the notion of a continuous learning process that may bridge *all* generations.

The emphasis on the allegedly necessary repression of the humanistic youth culture in favor of the more "rational" principles of modern society begs the question: "Industrial society for whom and/or for what purpose?" Because Parsons approaches the topic ahistorically, he overlooks the possibility that the society of today may very well carry within it the conditions of its own transformation (perhaps already begun) from industrial to postindustrial[29] society or, in political terms, perhaps (although without necessarily equating the two) from a democratic to a facist system.

Summary

Summing up the major characteristics of this type of explanation and its subtypes, we wish to emphasize once more that the students as subjects of the protest actions are generally seen as being in an exceptional situation—psychologically, socially, or in terms of age—one that either will naturally change into a "normal" state or that can be channeled into a direction acceptable to the dominant society. Two points are implicit in the writings of especially those authors who attribute protest actions to a pathological or in some way unbalanced personality: first, that the origin of an idea or action has a direct influence on its content and direction; and secondly, that "normal" behavior means being "acceptable" to existing society. That the idea of "normality" is not transhistorical but socially and culturally defined is rarely seen as a problem. Robert Coles is a noteworthy exception when he writes: "Not the least of our problems is that elusive idea, 'normal.' . . . Not the least of our problems is deciding what is 'sick' and what is 'healthy.' . . . We also have to worry about our own values, our own hopes and ideas of what is desirable for man, what helps him grow, and what is crippling and harmful."[30] In contrast to Coles, most of the other authors seem to take for granted that emphasis should be put on the system first and on the person second. The ideological character of this over-riding emphasis is clearly revealed in the "theoretical" argument that the young had better adjust to the system if they want to be counted among the "normal" adults.
But different values lead to different diagnoses. Christian Bay, for example, writes:

> The long-range rationality associated with 'intellectual' is also a broad-gauge rationality, moreover, in the sense that the intellectual recognizes his stake in an enlightened society and in enlightened citizenship on his own part. It is this propensity of the developed intellect that makes a rich and continuing supply of intellectuals not only an advantage but a necessity for a civilization if it is to survive in a complex and rapidly changing world.[31]

45

Bay, on the basis of his enlightened concept of university education, rejects the idea that the university should be an agent of a repressive socialization. To be critical of and rebel against repressive tendencies in and outside the educational institutions is for him the result of a rational education toward intellectual and personal independence as well as a successful resolution of ego-defensive and social-acceptance anxieties. According to him, "more conservative views, among students or adults generally, are likely to be less rationally, less independently motivated, compared to more radical-liberal views."[32]

The five psychologically oriented explanations of student protest imply three different proposals of conflict resolution: first, discipline must be reintroduced into the socialization and educational process. What has been suggested is a retrogression to more traditional values and education. Secondly, the structure and values of society must change toward a more humane and just state. The suggested avenues, depending on the political stance, call either for a radical transformation or a gradual progress of society in the light of its own utopian elements. Thirdly, psychiatrists must help students resolve their personal conflicts within their families or universities. Psychiatric treatment is to help students adjust to the *status quo* or to a status acceptable to the dominant society.

While the first and third suggestions seem to see the solution in an improved socialization process, the second one, at first glance, seems to accept the students' personalities as they are and take them as a standard for social criticism. Interestingly enough, however, the most important social scientists who took this sympathetic stance in the early days of the protest have since changed their minds. The change of heart, presumably, was a result of the impact of more radical and "extremist" types of action. Thus, Flacks and Keniston hold the lack of tolerance, wisdom, and "compassion for one's adversaries"[33] against the rebellious students and call upon the colleges and universities to help develop these qualities in the students. The same reversal occurred in the West German scenario. Habermas, while holding on to the hope that the student movement would provide a social-psychologically defined revolutionary potential in late capitalist systems, charged the West German SDS

46

in 1967 with "infantilism" and "fixed ideas" because students had allegedly equated the occupation of a campus with actual usurption of power in the larger society.[34] Thus, Habermas, once a Neomarxist, also ends up with a psychiatric vocabulary and thereby explains away the students' protest, albeit after students had used means not contained in the protest arsenal defined as proper by him.

4

THE POLITICAL TYPE

Political explanations, whether offered by the democratic pluralists or the Marxists, are generally derivative, for, although both see student protest as being played out in the political arena and through political processes, they view these actions as reflections of deep-rooted currents of conflict which permeate and affect society as a whole.

The Marxist explanation takes on its derivative coloration from its view of student protest as a manifestation of class conflict or of marginality status. In either case, whether as "new working class" or as "marginal group," students derive their position in the social structure from the new productive importance of the university in advanced capitalism. Because of this development, Marxists argue, students are the new agents of revolutionary change, and the student movement of the sixties in the United States and in other capitalist countries was a sign of their *engagément*. Marxist analysts, however, take great pains to point out that such actions, although manifested politically, are the result of class consciousness, and can be fully understood only in their relationship to society as a whole, more specifically, to the prevailing system of production. In view of this emphasis, we will consider them in our discussion of economically based explanations.

All other political explanatory explorations concerning American student unrest are generally guided by the precepts of what might best be called theory of democratic pluralism.* The social scientists who use this model argue that the political arena is a semiautonomous, self-sustaining subsystem with its own store of continuous occurrences and imperatives. In "open" democratic societies such as the United States, this political system has the function of mediating social tensions, tensions which are to be expected and in fact are a primary source of continual economic growth and expansion of liberty in democratic societies.[1] These tensions (which create special interests), and the working-out of their "public" resolution, provide the political system with a set of constraints and ideas. Political imperatives thus take on an existence all of their own. For these analysts, therefore, the political and public event of relatively rationally articulated and acted-upon interests is the locus of student protest. Such grievances or interests, they argue, stem rather naturally from their age-group and studenthood position, which legitimately should and do come into conflict with the positions of the faculty and university administration. Because democratic pluralist explanations, however, are concerned almost exclusively with interest clashes as they are revealed on the political marketplace, they are tied willy-nilly to *ex post facto* knowledge and analysis. It is for this reason, perhaps, that it took the mobilization of thousands of Berkeley students in 1964 and the rowdy, Luddite-like overturning of a police car before social scientists began to take this new and explicit source of social conflict seriously.

Once a protest—or more properly, in the terminology of democratic pluralism, a clash of interests—is perceived as having entered into the political process, it is imbued with meaning through the issues (both original and new) which become clarified in the ensuing debate and, which then are made subject to the constraints of the political system. These issues, in turn, may and often do give

* The theory of democratic pluralism includes both the "democratic power elite" and "interest-group pluralist" schools of thought. That very real differences between the two exist only becomes clear when the intent of the originators of these ideas is subjected to scrutiny. Floyd Hunter and C. Wright Mills, for example, came to believe that there was a growing concentration of power in certain groups in the United States and used their information as a debunking device in order to alert their colleagues and others to the passing of participatory democracy.

rise to interest groups that see themselves affected by the way in which they may be resolved. "Power" at this level is defined as the amount of pressure the various groups can bring to bear on protecting their particular interests, while "issues" define the conflict and often the anticipated type of mobilization for action and counteraction. The focus is primarily on the *content* of a particular issue or set of issues, and the analysis may become extremely sophisticated and complex, depending on the intensity, size, duration, and the possible kindling of other political grievances. Student unrest, for example in its first dramatic outcropping at Berkeley, was considered a local clash over a specific interpretation of the "rules of the game," and therefore, according to Seymour Lipset and Philip Altbach, nothing more than a contained low-level political event because it had no immediate or similar repercussions on other college campuses.[2] Since then, of course, student unrest has preoccupied a generation of social scientists, many of whom have enlarged their concern to include the black and urban protest movements. For most of these social analysts, however, basic *causes* of student unrest remain, "on the other side" of the political fence; that is, except for legitimately articulated perceptions and needs, they view them as lying outside the university. The assumption is that the university is much the same as the political system, a semiautonomous institution with its own imperatives and continuous history whatever its links to outside society. Hence, they look for the causes of student protest, as well as all other protests, in the very nature of society. For this reason, democratic-pluralist explanations are by their very nature derivative, a characteristic they share with those of Marxist persuasion. The difference between the two lies in their starting points: for the former, the search is conducted within the boundaries of the democratic-industrial social system, while the latter's search is focused on the historical development of changing societal arrangements. History, however, is not ignored by democratic-pluralist writers, it merely enters their discussions at a different level and serves a different purpose. Since most of these writers are committed to a positivistic methodology, issue analysis serves as the instrumentality through which consensual processes or political trends

51

may be "discovered" and "predicted," so that possible resolutions to conflicts of interests may be "prescribed." At this level, process—a development of an issue or issues over time—which is the empirical substitute for historical analysis, is usually introduced through the application of a collective behavioral approach. Related events are thus "followed through" to their final success or failure. It is not surprising, therefore, that social scientists are still not sure whether the collected series of student protests in the past decade were (or still are) a movement, a rebellion, a revolution, merely a high-intensity period in the eternal generation gap, or the result of continual technical revolutions.

In their efforts to explore these external political causes of student unrest, some analysts suggest that they are internally generated by irrationally experienced emotions related to the needs of late adolescents in a highly industrialized mass society, while others view unrest as being triggered by external societal pressures such as the Vietnam war, the urban crisis, and black militance.[3] Some writers attribute even deeper motives to student protest, especially when attempting to explain the New Left. Philip Altbach, for instance, suggests that the political actions of these students are inspired by a feeling of "historical mission," to achieve goals which the older generation failed to achieve.[4] Whatever the suggested cause, pluralist social scientists are generally agreed that the form of student protest has two faces: withdrawal or *engagément*, passivity or activism. They talk of culturally alienated youth[5]—hippies, freakouts, yippies, etc.—and young people who are politically active.[6] Political explanations naturally center on the young who operate on the political market place, and of those, especially on the visible "activist." Although political explanations do not concern themselves directly with the counterculture youth group, they do recognize its importance as a source of potentially mobilizable persons who can be (and are) often called upon by the politicized activist.[7]

Within the democratic framework of interest-group explanations, the inherent correctness or incorrectness of student "demands" and "issues," as well as the methods employed to further their cause, assumes overriding importance. The logic dictating the standard of "correctness," although expressed in different ways, is as follows: due process (a basic tenet of democracy) in the (liberal) university relies on rationality, the nature and direction of which is derived from the "effective pursuit, discovery, publication and teaching of the truth."[8] This academic due process is authoritative (as opposed to due process in the political community, with whom academic shares this notion) and dependent on the teacher's range of knowledge and depth of experience. In this authoritative community, students and faculty are equals as questioners and participants because of the "rule of reason," therefore, for students to raise the question or issue of educational reform is inherently correct, that is, legitimate, and sometimes very necessary.[9] Lipset, Kristol, Howe, and Feuer,[10] although altering the specifics in minor ways (some tend toward the historical, others toward the developmental), all agree that there is merit in student dissent and legitimacy in their interests. But, when the academic-reason game is disrupted by the presentation of, for example, nonnegotiable demands (black students excepted because of their history), confrontation, strikes, or violence, they are also agreed that the authoritative dictum must be enforced. Hook takes an extreme position on this dictum, but it is little different from the others. In his view, "The peculiar deficiency of the ritualistic liberal educational establishment is the failure to meet violations of rational due process with appropriate sanctions." For, it is clear, he says, that "whoever interferes with academic due process either by violence or threat of violence places himself outside the academic community, and incurs the sanctions appropriate to the gravity of his offense, from censure to suspension to expulsion."[11] Hook faults faculties and administrations for their failure to recognize and punish the very first infractions of the use of non-student interest-group issues like war, racism, and poverty, and the uses of noncompromisable methods, because they stem from undemocratic sets of values. In his opinion this lack of vigilance is responsible for the escalation and changed character of student demands and the ever-increasing use of violent rule-breaking tactics. Lipset and Altbach offer yet another sector to share the blame. The mass media, they claim, in their eagerness for the news' story highlight confrontation—especially the gory ones—educate and

53

spread the message of illegitimate and irrational dissent.[12]

These reactive, instrumental causal explanations tend to negate the student *per se* as subject and focus primarily on those objective elements which appear to depart from the model outlined above. Any substantive questioning of the model itself that may be behind the "issues" is side-stepped by declaring them out of bounds. Mass media make for irrationality and emotional responses rather than tolerant contemplative listening and compromise. Illegitimate demands and confrontation smack of deviant and dysfunctional norms and disrupt the basic cohesiveness of common values necessary to democratic solutions. The larger society has responded to the student attack on traditional institutions by emphasizing law and order; in the university the response has been, although not forceful enough in the opinion of some, censure, suspension, and the calling in of civil authorities. In the larger society there have been some "reasonable" reforms: broader social-service benefits, housing, quicker processing of accused persons, and a plan of troop with-drawal from Vietnam. Inside the university there has been an attempt to make the curriculum more relevant, to change the teaching style, and to provide for greater student participation. Force and reason tinged with benign neglect have been the proposed solutions explicit or implicit in the instrumental causal explanations offered by social scientists as well as politicians. Implied is the assumption that with some minor rearrangements and a judicial use of force, the democratic-pluralist model can be reset into its proper orbit.

Because the democratic pluralistic model has for long been the principal source of social-science theory in the United States, and because the problems of democratic development are fundamental to an understanding of the student protest (and all other protests of the past decade), it would seem advisable to sketch the precepts and construction of this model in ideal-typical terms.

The theory departs from the belief that "individual worth" is best served by individual competition, which, in turn, serves the commonweal. While continued progress is assured by the balance forged by compromise solutions of tensions that naturally arise because of the different needs of individuals, the mechanism of providing equal opportunity tends to mitigate the obvious fact that people are not born equal in talent, intelligence, station, or race, and offers everyone the possibility of participating in the formulation of solutions to commonly held societal problems, be they economic, social, or political. Translated into political terms, individuals become "the public." It is within the public sector that problems become sharpened and are examined on the grounds of an agreed set of core values, tolerance, and honest discussion based on the knowledge of the facts of the matter.[13] Individuals are thus enabled to break the bonds of class ties, of ethnic and racial differences as well as regionally induced interests. In a representative democracy such as the United States, the debate over the definition of problems and their possible solutions may be among the "elite," but their power and legitimacy is drawn from "the public." Thus, interest-group theory which is based on this conception holds that everybody can participate in the general political decision-making process through voting and/or membership in organized pressure groups. It is with this conception of reality that student protesters differ widely, arguing, by their taking to the streets as well as in their self-analysis, that their needs and societal interests do not have a chance of being articulated and represented within the institutional framework (interest groups, parties or pressure groups, etc.), and that before their use of confrontational tactics their interests were not being seriously considered or dealt with by the polity.

This theory of democratic pluralism has become a fully articulated model only since World War II. During this period, three complementary ideas were developed in the American social sciences. The first two were derived from a conference held in Rome in 1955 on "The Future of Freedom,"* at which intellectuals and social scientists were brought together to discuss the meaning of ideology and utopia in the free world. Their common interest seems to have been based on a profound political and personal disaffection with Left politics.[14] The third idea was home-grown.

The first of these ideas is best expressed in Daniel Bell's *The End of*

---

* The meeting held between September 12 and 17, 1955 in Rome, was organized by the Congress for Cultural Freedom. The Congress was later exposed to be a front organization of the CIA. Among the American participants were Daniel Bell, Seymour M. Lipset, Kenneth Galbraith, George Kennan, Arthur Schlesinger, Jr., Sidney Hook, and Frederick A. Hayek.

Ideology,[15] published in 1960, in which he outlines the normative ideas and historical underpinnings of a new set of parameters within which political decision-making was currently taking place. These new parameters, he argues, are the product of the alienation and destruction of the extremes of both Left and Right in political discourse.

Only at the extremes, he writes, can ideological debates take place, as in the case of nineteenth century Europe where politics was the arena of an ardent ideological dialogue about the meaning and basis of democratic life. It was conducted between the world view of a still vibrant and revolutionary capitalism and its antithesis, socialism; the protagonists were the new bourgeois and the "intellectual." The latter, according to Bell, because of his special status position and his reliance on a free-floating type of experiential sensibility, "felt that the wrong values were being honored, and rejected society" (p. 372). In search for "his truth," the "intellectual" embarked on the "faith ladder" in which the "vision of the future cannot distinguish possibilities from probabilities, and converts the latter into certainties," and so he [the intellectual] became an extreme Left "ideologue," a utopian socialist. By defining ideology as "an all-inclusive system of comprehensive reality . . . a set of beliefs, infused with passion," which "seeks to transform the whole of a way of life,"[16] and by infusing it with the myopia engendered by a confusion of practical possibilities and probable outcomes, Bell points out that the position held by the Left was exhausted and made into a falsehood by the calamities of Soviet socialism. From the moment of this unfrocking of a flawed utopia, he continues, "left ideology" lost its "truth" and its power to persuade, teaching its former adherents not to "risk the sacrifice of the present generation for a future that may see only a new exploitation by a new elite."[17] The knowledge gained, however, was that "if old debates are meaningless, some old verities are not—verities of free speech, free press, and the right of opposition and of free inquiry."[18]

Puritan capitalism, on the other hand, he says, has also mellowed. In the course of time it incorporated the Left's ideas of social welfare and the desirability of decentralized power, which, taken together, have made for a system of mixed economy and political pluralism.

The practicality of the bourgeois, along with the debunking of the Soviet system, Bell concludes, has deprived the Left of a meaningful place in the political decision-making process of modern-day society. Political pluralism is thus a reality based on historical necessity, while the intellectual, a person who thrives on extremes, is somehow a historical vestige—a modern-day *lumpen*.

The second idea, this one also in the form of a book, surfaced that same year, 1960. Building on the concept of Bell's disappearing parameters, Seymour M. Lipset, in *Political Man*, argued that political decision-making in the Western capitalist democracies was now centered on commonly defined and accepted problems, the solutions of which were primarily dependent on the ability of society to mobilize its forces and its technological capabilities. This was so, he continued, pushing Bell's argument a bit further, because "the fundamental political problems of the industrial revolution have been solved,"[19] while the democratic social revolution had ended the need for "ideological" impetus for political action. Even more important, and still following Bell's thesis, he points out that on the basis of empirical evidence, the class-conflict potential envisioned by left intellectuals has been substantially reduced by the decline of absolute deprivation under welfare capitalism. Therefore, on the basis of empirical evidence, he finds that he can declare "democracy is not only the way to seek the good society; it is the good society itself in operation" (p. 403).

Although, writes Lipset, there is a lessening of interest in political inquiry in democratic societies (for on the domestic scene the public is involved with the more technical problem-solving business of making a good thing better), intellectual passion and search for utopian truth still have a place in the realm of world politics, especially in the underdeveloped world. There, the new "ideology" of the West has yet to fulfill its modernizing and utopian function. The "intellectual," now in a university setting, is still the font of the "mission." In new nations, Lipset contends, the university is one of the principal agencies of modernizing traditional societies, and thus the carrier of the new ideology. It follows from this that students in these universities may be expected to (and must) engage in radical politics and "ideological" debates. Students in already democratized modern societies, however, empirically do not have to (and theoretically ought not to) play this same role. Thus, Lipset concludes, if American students desert the legitimate realm of public problem-solving to debate and act upon fundamental issues (which in fact have been solved) and do not submit to learning the instrumentalities of democratic decision-making and to advancing technical know-how, they have been improperly socialized, or, even more tragically, they have misread their true historical role.

The third development, much in line with the above two, provided the necessary instrument needed to link these larger societal theoretical and analytical concerns with the agency of their institutionalization. This involved the spelling-out of the changed nature and role of the university. It is perhaps not by chance alone that this linkage was provided for by the former president of one of the largest universities in the United States—the University of California—Dr. Clark Kerr, a man who has long concerned himself with the relationship between industry and education. In his Godkin Lectures[20] at Harvard University, delivered in April, 1963, Dr. Kerr outlined the connection in his answers to two crucial questions which he posed to himself: (1) What is the role of university education in a highly industrialized democratic society? and (2) What are the characteristic and necessary shape, form, and function of the university *qua* institution if it is to fulfill its changed educational role?

It is in his answers that democratic pluralism was first given the substance within which most political explanations of student protest are subsumed. The university, he posited, occupies a unique position and a new centrality in our society. This, he claimed, is due to the "wide-spread recognition that new knowledge is the most important factor in economic and social growth" and that the university's "invisible product, knowledge, may be the most powerful single factor in our culture, affecting the rise and fall of professions and even of social classes, of regions and even of nations."[21] Since 1963, this idea has been more fully elaborated. Daniel Bell argues, for example, that the new centrality of universities turns on "what has now become decisive for society . . . the new centrality of theoretical knowledge, the primacy of theory over empiricism, and the codification of knowledge into abstract systems of symbols that can be translated into many different and varied circumstances."[22] Thus, "it is theoretical knowledge that has become the matrix of innovation"[23] and the university its primary agency. Kerr, on his part, envisioned the transformed American university not only as a unique model because it developed out of American processes and history, but also as a futuristic model. The multi-versity became the model of a model university.

For Kerr, the multiversity reflects and is at one with society. In his words, it "has become a prime instrument of national purpose,"[24] and this is what makes it new and right. Its power base has moved from "inside to outside," and power now resides in the public authority. The multiversity has many "publics" which are fractionalized—students, faculty, the state, private donors, alumni, and administrators—as does the larger society. It has to answer the call for massive education by all groups and all interests. It is therefore large, as is the society that carries it. To the multiversity "progress is more important than peace,"[25] and this too reflects American society of the sixties. The president of the university is manager of the "city-state," as is the president of the United States of the nation-state. The multiversity mirrors the total society in that as a total system it is "extraordinarily flexible, decentralized, competitive and productive."[26] And finally, he points out, "pluralism in higher education matches the pluralistic American society . . . (it) is the child of middle-class pluralism."[27] Thus, he reasons, if students are irritated by the machinery of the multiversity, it simply reflects the alienation of the larger society due to mechanization and bigness, one of the major "problems" that both the university and society must (and will) solve. For as American society seeks the good and great society, so does the university, through the professional offices of the social scientist and humanist. These domestic "intellectuals" will, it is hoped, "define the good as well as the true and add wisdom to truth."[28]

Just as there are differences among groups of individuals on the basis of occupation, closeness to the centers of decision-making, life-styles, etc., so there are differences in the community of universities. As Lipset so aptly puts it, "the primary function of the university is scholarship, which includes rigorous education, not politics or therapy ... there can only be a relatively small number of universities which have severe standards for faculty and students, although there will be thousands of accredited institutions of higher education."[29] According to this construction, the elitism of the university—albeit an elite of merit—inherent in the hierarchical nature of the institution is buttressed by the new postindustrial needs of the public. Although legitimacy still rests in the public and ultimate power with the politician, the polity has long since accepted elite leadership in policy matters because of the complexity of social relations and the importance of technically oriented public debate. The seeming contradiction between the institutionalization of meritocracy in the university, elite politics, and the concept of a populist democratic society had already been resolved by Daniel Bell, who had so adroitly shown that both these groups operate in an environment dedicated to an egalitarian philosophy. And it was confirmed by Lipset, who argued that since class interests were mitigated, interest groups and elite groups had fluid membership which insured and stimulated the egalitarian nature of public debate and of society.

Student unrest, as well as other forms of protest, have called into question the two mainstays of the democratic-pluralistic model: its legitimation of the *status quo* (i.e., the good society) and its ability to foreclose other alternatives. The uses of the university, especially in "old" developed nations, have been found wanting. For student war protesters, peace *is* progress, at least so runs the rhetoric. The concept of "progress" itself has, for student activists and counter-culture youth (the new intellectuals?), become the rallying point of passion and the search for "truth." Democratic pluralists have been hard put to explain the rejection of disappearing limits, and they have sought the causes in the softness of permissive socialization, the destruction of academic freedom, the generation gap, and democratic society overstepping its own bounds—of too much, too soon. The utopian elements of the American Ideal—"equality, liberty, and justice for all," individual free will and equal opportunity—which democratic pluralists accepted as the accomplished constants of their model are the very elements which have been used in the quest for alternatives: communes, a redefinition of participatory democracy, an attack on elitism, and a redefinition of the uses and structure of the university. The explanations offered by students, at least in the words of the slogans and argumentations offered by student writers in the mass of literature that they have published as well as in the lives they have chosen to lead, are ample evidence of their disaffection. The fact that theorists of democratic pluralism have denied this disaffection as symptomatic of a genuine search for social and political change by labeling those in the forefront "the lunatic fringe," "extremists," "freaks," etc., merely exposes them to questions concerning their own ideological biases.

5

THE
ECONOMIC
MODE

In response to the accelerated rate of scientific and technical innovation and the rise of automation, cybernetics and electronics, often referred to as the third industrial revolution, leading social scientists have developed the concept of "postindustrial society," to account for these changes. This view of current American society grew out of an earlier consensus among social scientists in the 1950s that the new industrialism had neutralized the parameters of opposing socio-economic systems, that the capitalist and socialist forms of society had indeed converged. The internal development of either system was seen as determined by the necessary adjustments to a permanent technological revolution unfolding according to the immanent and quasi-autonomous progress of science.[1] Accepting the outward economic picture of the post-World-War II period at face value, these writers believed that the labor force was well integrated into the productive system and that class struggle in its traditional sense had ceased. Taking cognizance of the new stage of capitalist organization that had begun in the Great Depression, and focusing on the necessity to include the internal consumer market, social scientists interpreted conflicts as being one-sidely caused solely by problems of distribution and access.*

On the basis of this conglomerate of ideas, plus Kerr's notion of the "centrality" of knowledge in the multiversity, Daniel Bell has suggested that the newly emerging postindustrial society will be dependent on the intellectual leadership of the universities, which will assume eminent importance in the productive sector. Abstract and theoretical knowledge that can be applied to many different, yet not historically unique situations, he claims, "has become the matrix of innovation."[2] While policy decisions will remain in the governmental realm for some time to come, they will become increasingly technical in nature and hence depend more and more on technical expertise. In such a way, universities—the home of experts—will become a major participant in policy-making. In fact, Bell concludes, the intellectual realm will become so dominant in the postindustrial society that "the entire complex of social prestige and social status will be rooted in the intellectual and scientific communities" (p. 30).

Advocates of the theory of postindustrial society hold that the initiative for social change rests with technical elites and that the transition from industrial to postindustrial society can legitimately be called a revolution. It is not surprising therefore that student protest appears to them as counterrevolutionary, an anticipatory conflict sparked by an "obsolete youth"[3] (centered in the humanities and social sciences) interested in expressive values and humanism which run contrary to the technical organization of the larger society. If this is to be taken as an explanation of student protest, several glaring deficiencies question its validity. First of all, the conception seems to include only the so-called counterculture and its proponents, without taking into account what Keniston has called politically involved activists. Secondly, students of the humanities and social sciences could be termed expendable only if a postindustrial society could do without planning, coordination, education, and creation of legitimations. Bell's own descriptions and

* The neutralization of the conflict potential of the productive sector was associated with the new practice of subsuming fascism (and Nazism) and communism under the rubric of totalitarianism, which was aided and abetted by the general anticommunist and anti-Soviet predisposition of the era.

extrapolations, however, negate this. Finally, the content of the students' issues and demands is not discussed in its own right but instead is viewed from a purely functional perspective, while student social criticism is turned into a disutility.

Some American social scientists do not hold with the "neutral" character of U.S. society, but on the contrary explicitly recognize and underline the continued viability, flexibility, and even supe-riority of the capitalist system. Peter Berger,[4] for example, predicts that the conflict between the youth culture and the "bureaucratic establishments," both in and outside the university, will be resolved by a hierarchical differentiation among the universities.* The "liberated" undergraduate campuses will be the loci of the youth culture, constituting "immense T-groups" without any economic relevance, while the interests of government and industry will be catered to by special graduate schools and professional institutes.

More recently, Peter and Brigitte Berger have added that the still viable Protestant ethic remains a prime organizing factor.[5] They predict that if leftist student protesters continue to reject this ethic, American society will recruit its useful members from the more traditional strata—ethnic minorities and low-income groups still interested in upward social mobility. According to the Bergers, this potential source of willing and trainable white-collar labor force (and it is a sizable number) will eventually have the major effect of downward mobility for the student rebels should these continue their "great refusal."

At the institutional level, non-Marxists are quick to focus on the students' resentment of the internal pressures in the multiversities resulting from dehumanizing bureaucracies, bigness, anomie, etc. Although they recognize with a sense of regret and resignation that the multiversity has become reality, they cling to the belief that the university should be a place of detached scholarship. That the protest against the multiversity is carried on by "irrational" and "emotional"[6] students desiring humane treatment is either viewed with slight cynicism (Berger) or with a critical undertone (Bell). Facing up to reality, no matter how harsh and painful it may be,

---

* On this point Berger concurs with Lipset's prediction. Cf. Chapter Four, p. 60, and footnote 29.

most members of academe accept the multiversity as "the reality taken for granted."[1]

During the same period that the social-science establishment was concerned with either proclaiming the continued viability of American capitalism or mystifying U.S. society by negating its capitalist principle, the neo-Marxist social philosopher Herbert Marcuse was discussing the possibilities of qualitative change in industrial societies. However, he too did not foresee that unrest would be sparked in the student intellectual sector in the early sixties.[8] This failure can be attributed to his agreement—down to terminology—with the theorists of postindustrial society on the basic characteristics of advanced "industrial" (not *capitalist!*) society, particularly the role of science and technology. Elaborating on the old Frankfurt School theme of science as domination,[9] Marcuse in *One-Dimensional Man* argued that technological rationality had become the paramount oppressive force in modern society, providing the possibility for both the containment of disintegrating tendencies and the potential for a rupture of history and development of a "free" society. Accepting the thesis that the proletariat had been integrated into the one-dimensional system[10] and describing the American society of the fifties and early sixties as a false totality—as the negation of the "good life"—Marcuse suggested that qualitative social change could only occur as the negation of the negation, that is, as a transformation of the whole from the outside—carried by the excluded "underclass" on the one hand, and some philosophically enlightened individuals on the other. Marcuse's renunciation of political economic categories and analysis in *One-Dimensional Man* made him the captive of the same surface phenomena so eloquently praised by his bourgeois colleagues. His "critical" approach, thus, turned into a mystique, wavering between the "total" and the "totally different,"[11] and negating internal societal contradictions by accepting appearances.

Despite our fundamental disagreement with Marcuse's approach in *One-Dimensional Man*, however, we recognize the importance of some of his basic concerns and the validity of parts of his social critique of present-day reality in both capitalist and socialist systems. For Marcuse, as well as for us, the disquieting question is how men who are deeply affected and "perverted" by the "false" nature of Western societies can turn into revolutionary subjects and become "free" individuals even before the arrival of a "free" society, a society which would bear no resemblance to the petrified systems of the current socialist bureaucracies but rather be "a work of art."[12] In his formulation of the proposition, the "dialectics of liberation" has to set in at the individual level, at the level of the repressed and arrested potential of "the mind *and* the body, reason *and* imagination, the intellectual *and* instinctual levels."[13] Thus, educators as part of the intelligentsia, who "by virtue of their privileged position, can pierce the ideological and material veil of mass communication and indoctrination,"[14] adopt an especially important function in the struggle for liberation. In 1968, Marcuse attributed to the intelligentsia "a decisive preparatory function," but "not more," for he did not see the intelligentsia as a revolutionary class in and of itself. But at the same time he did take notice of the "increasingly scientific character of the material process of production,"[15] a theme further developed in a later work,[16] where he has suggested that the ever-increasing intellectualization of the work force carries with it the chance that more and more people would eventually join the struggle for change.

Under the impact of the protest actions organized around ascribed status groups in the U.S. and of neocolonial liberation struggles, Marcuse's earlier version about the revolutionary potential in the marginal sectors of society has been taken up and developed into what can be called the "peripheral theory."[17] Like the thesis of postindustrial society, this proposition starts with the assumption that the productive center is functioning smoothly and no longer generates conflicts that reverberate throughout society, as Old Left theory had postulated. On the contrary, so the argument runs, "in the present stage of advanced industrial society, the crisis is on the periphery, not at the center";[18] blacks, women, and students tend to be most affected by the relative underdevelopment of the public sector, prompting them to take up various forms of protest. Therefore a qualitative change of the whole system may possibly be brought about by all marginal groups, as, demanding access to the system separately but simultaneously, they overwhelm it. Implied in this thesis is the notion that technological progress increases the number of expendable people and makes it ever more difficult for the system to accommodate all who seek access.

If "peripheral theory" is to be considered Neomarxian, it confuses the level of appearances with the essence of advanced capitalist society. Protest by marginal groups is equated with the crisis of capitalism. The theory assumes—without empirical demonstration—a fixed correspondence of objectively given structural contradictions and protest potential, where these contradictions become manifest as social conflicts. Advocates of this position also postulate that protest resulting from these conflicts will lead to a resolution of the objectively existing contradictions in capitalism. They do not answer, however, to the questions why a certain contradiction should manifest itself only in form of certain conflicts, or why certain conflicts should lead to a resolution of basic contradictions.[19]

In peripheral theory, as in the theories about the end-of-ideology and postindustrial society, the productive center of society is encapsulated and cut off from the distributive and consumptive sectors, thereby breaking up the totality and interconnectedness of the economic system. Even more important, however, is the absence of theoretical differentiation between and conceptual definition of the various bases of marginality and their relation to the revolutionary potential. Lacking this theoretical clarity, peripheral theory becomes a hodgepodge of empirical observations with a dash of derivates from New Left theory. Despite these deficiencies, it cannot be denied, however, that peripheral theory and its more fully developed antecedent, dependency theory[20] (elaborated by Latin American social scientists), and similar theses about disparity and social conflicts in late capitalist systems advanced by some members of the Frankfurt School, including Marcuse, can claim a certain plausibility. They need, however, more theoretical elaboration and empirical investigation.

It has already become obvious from our discussion that Neomarxian analysts are not fully agreed upon the basis and nature of student protest nor the potential source of a qualitative transformation of American society. A major disagreement lies in the following: while Marcuse and others have viewed the students primarily as a *vanguard* of a yet indeterminate mass movement, other authors have proposed that protesting students have been most effective when they acted as a class in and of itself—when they have been true to themselves and expressed their own repressed needs and interests most impressively exemplified by the French student revolt of 1968. In their critical assessment of the American SDS during the sixties, Greg Calvert and Carol Neiman,[21] for example, reject the idea of poverty or race as possible sources for radical social change in the United States. Because they are not part of the productive process, marginal groups, in their view, are the least likely to develop a socialist perspective. They argue instead that the revolutionary potential must be sought in line with the structural changes of the labor force resulting from the needs of the "neocapitalist" system to ensure rising profits and consumption, avoid overproduction, and maintain labor as a source of income despite the "historic potential of our era" for a "society of 'post-scarcity' and fully automated production" (p. 78). Students are defined by them as "pre-workers" or members of the "new working class," who, as the college-trained population rapidly increases, learn painfully that they are no longer guaranteed the entry into the American middle class (in its consumerism aspect). For, they argue, the educational system has been turned into a track system, intimating that the internal differentiation between intellectuals in terms of their diverse functions (e.g., management, planning, coordination, research, education, legitimation) has been complemented by a more rigid hierarchical structuring of their socioeconomic status. Calvert and Neiman, however, base their argument on a linear projection of a steady decrease of the unskilled in the productive sector, without fully exploring the effects of modern production techniques on the work situation. Automation, for example, tends to downgrade many skilled workers, shifting them to newly created jobs which often do not require special skills. In fact, there are indications that in automated production processes, conflict potential develops because of a growing polarization between the new class of overqualified unskilled workers at the bottom and the technical intelligentsia at the top.[22]

In general, Neomarxists see the emergence of the multiversity as a structural vehicle for the heightened social necessity of a specific program of indoctrination. And it is especially in the realm of higher education that the new "class position" of the students first came into sharper focus. Students can then be characterized as being more and more a "major exploited class" whose intelligence, training, and work is being used for purposes beyond their control and against their interests. It is their working conditions and their "miserable" situation within the "productive" process of the university that create the condition of alienation in the classical Marxian sense and account for their revolutionary potential.[23]

The Neomarxists use the descriptions of the new uses of the university offered by their protagonists to support their criticism. They agree with Bell and others that the university has assumed a "quasi-monopoly in determining the future stratification system of society."[24] For them, Kerr's multiversity, with its emphasis on instrumental learning, technical training, and servicing the national community, does epitomize the modern university. The fact that the university has assumed an important economic function in modern technological society has led to a situation in which a specific set of economic principles—competitive achievement, possessive individualism, and the prompt delivery of measurable performance—has caused a change in the self-perception, norms, and goals of the university community. Both sides—Neomarxists and their protagonists—are agreed that the university has become a business corporation. As such, the university follows the marketplace dictum: the bigger the plant and the number of customers served, the more diverse its structure and the more publics it has, the greater its economic worth. But Neomarxists contend, the "price" paid is the university's loss of critical distance from society, exemplified in its research services to the military-industrial complex.

The new uses of the university, it appears to us, have set into motion a series of paradoxical situations: on the one hand, modern society demands an increasingly larger pool of knowledgeable labor which the university has agreed to train and deliver; on the other hand, however, the technological system is not ready to use the entire "supply," so that part of this "readied" labor must be kept off the "market" at any given moment. Moreover, the economic system, operating on the classical economic notion that there has to be expendable labor (oversupply) so that the relatively most capable may be hired and their labor cost kept low, confronts the university with a dilemma: new techniques and advancing technology tend to make its graduates expendable at the moment of certification—the problem of obsolescence amidst overproduction. This refers to students of the traditional humanistic subjects (as the postindustrial theorists contend), but even more so to science and engineering students.

Graduates of elite universities are in greatest demand because they are considered the most capable and their schools among the major sources of scientific-technical innovation. The vast majority of colleges by contrast serves the purpose of keeping students off the labor market as long as possible, while at the same time training them for and "making" them accept positions at the lower end of the occupational hierarchy. This disparity in the educational sector reflects an asymmetrical development in the larger society: the contrast between life chances of different social classes and the uneven development of the various realms of daily life encountered by the same individual. This dual disparity, according to Neomarxist sociologists, causes conflicts, especially at the periphery of the system, that is, in those sectors not directly related to the industrial productive process and among those groups who are either totally excluded from the productive center of society or only indirectly linked to it—the poor, the unemployed, the ethnic minorities. Students, who as a group are not yet integrated into society, some claim,[25] experience the relative underdevelopment of the educational sector and are subject to "peripheral" tensions. But because of their education, they are probably more able to articulate these "felt" tensions and likely to comprehend them as the result of the contradictions inherent in advanced capitalism.

Although Neomarxists hold that the conflict will be resolved only through a radical transformation of Western societies, they do not predict an imminent revolution. On the contrary, they attribute only a very limited conflict potential to the current student

71

movement. This movement will pose a serious threat to the system only if the students win the support of the majority inside and outside the campus through mass enlightenment, as Habermas suggests or in the long run through the increasing intellectualization and concomitant proletarization of the intelligentsia, as Marcuse argues. In the latter case, intellectual work becomes alienated labor in the large bureaucratic institutions where technicians work on the solution to limited problems rather than realizing their creative potential as intellectuals.

Some are even more skeptical. Capitalism has so far demonstrated great flexibility and ability to cope with all serious threats by its willingness to make adjustments and compromises as long as its basic identity is not questioned. Marcuse's earlier pessimism* about the eventually fascist reactions of the system remains a serious consideration. In France, for example, Alan Touraine foresees the development of corporate capitalism based on a gigantic centralized bureaucracy which regulates people's lives in terms of welfare, work, and leisure.[26]

To sum up the Neomarxist position: student protest is explained as resulting from contradictions arising in the economic sphere and defined as having a potential, however small, of bringing about a radical social change in the future. Whether this potential will eventually be realized depends on a variety of conditions and developments. Since theirs is a critical theory of society geared to political praxis, these developments and conditions are continuously identified, examined, and evaluated by them.

* Cf. *One-Dimensional Man.*

6

THE
CULTURAL
MATRIX

There is a revolution coming. It will not be like revolutions of
the past. It will originate with the individual and with culture,
and it will change the political structure only as its final act. It
will not require violence to succeed, and it cannot be successfully resisted by violence. It is now spreading with amazing
rapidity, and already our laws, institutions and social structure
are changing in consequence. It promises a higher reason, a
more human community, and a new and liberated individual.
Its ultimate creation will be a new and enduring wholeness and
beauty—a renewed relationship of man to himself, to other men,
to society, to nature, and to the land.
This is the revolution of the new generation. Their protest and
rebellion...

CHARLES REICH—
The Greening of America[1]

Explorations in new musical sounds, art, and literary forms, total
immersion in sensate and aesthetic experiences, experiments in
psychic expansion, discoveries of new "needs" and new self-aware-
ness, attempts to organize new communal structures and experiments in political *engagément* are nothing more than another set of
unusual fads fashioned by another young generation. The young are
always rebellious and chiliastic—at least so argue those social

scientists who use the generation-gap thesis to explain what they see as the overwrought reaction or downright petulant violence of the Woodstock generation. But an equally vocal group of mod-scene interpreters sees in these efforts an attempt to reverse the "escape from freedom" road taken by a corrupt society which has turned its back on the American Dream. They see in the counterculture not a simple, isolated American response, but a historic rupture with the very traditions and mores of Western civilization. In answer to would-be detractors of the youth culture who vainly seek a well-thought-out set of programs and a theoretically constructed set of goals, these sympathetic commentators are quick to point out that although the "movement" may have begun with acts of individual negation, youth's reactions to the continuing crisis of American life have long since become more than mere rebellion. Not yet resolved either in science or politics, however, is the question of whether, in fact, the new generation's "psychic need to assert itself" has been spent (or sufficiently satisfied) so that some degree of normalcy can be reestablished without changing basic societal structures, or whether "negation has turned to revolution" which will not stop short of changes of a qualitative nature. This irresolution persists despite attempts to convert philosophical and moral differences into mere technical difficulties or to declare the "youth problem" done with because college campuses have returned to calm and reasoned discussion, and the youth to more socially acceptable issues. Settled or not, however, the issues spurred a broader and more fundamental questioning of the doctrines and practices of American society concerning equality, marginality, equity, and even routine day-to-day living.

Although Charles Reich is not the most typical exponent of the cultural interpretation, he was for a time its poet laureate. Thus it is fitting that we should again turn to him for the essence of the counterculture's potential as he and those like him see it.

> [The revolution] is both necessary and inevitable, and in time, it will include not only youth, but all people in America...

> The meaning and the future of the revolution emerge from a perspective on America. The revolution is a movement to bring man's thinking, his society, and his life to terms with the

revolution of technology and science that has already taken place. Technology demands of man a new mind—a higher, transcendent reason—if it is to be controlled and guided rather than to become an unthinking monster...

At the heart of everything is ... a change of consciousness. This means a "new head"—a new way of living—a new man [pp. 2–3].

The point of departure of the-greening-of-America thesis is that desires for change spring from and concern the national culture itself. Thus, change must be revolutionary because of the nature of its locus and its carriers. For Reich and others of his persuasion, the counterculture is inevitable, reasonable, and painfully necessary because the young are not only breaking with the present but also with the past. The "movement," then, is more radical and all-encompassing than any America has as yet experienced.

Underlying the cultural explanations is the contention that student protest—the political expression of the "new" transcendency—and the youth culture reside and are manifested in the realms of values, beliefs, and Weltanschauungen. The cultural sphere is perceived to be a self-contained entity, and major emphasis is placed on the initiating role of culture as the medium through which meaning is created and changed. Culture, therefore, is viewed as an independent rather than dependent variable.

In the main, writers who advance this type of explanation differ greatly from those considered in the preceding chapters. Generally called "social critics" or "social commentators," they too are professionals, but they usually occupy the twilight zone between the so-called hard-core social sciences and the humanities. They have strong attachments to the traditions of philosophic and poetic license which, while reinforcing their academic marginality, also characteristically permit them to transcend the neat but stifling pigeonholes of the standard disciplines. Although their interpretations, as one might expect, tend to defy social-science categories, we have included their analyses of student protest because they should be afforded the social-science credibility they deserve. Their merit in this regard is twofold. For one, they address realities which in one form or another have been both recognized and investigated by

75

social scientists attempting to explain student dissent,[2] and second-ly, they echo (and have popularized) the growing consensus in the social sciences on the need for an interdisciplinary or synthesizing view of society and have transmitted the air of urgency accompanying this agreement.* Unlike many American social scientists who are trying to develop a universalistic theory of society based on the interconnectedness of ostensibly quasi-autonomous spheres of personality, culture, and the social system, these critics have invoked their license to move freely betwixt and between these supposedly distinct analytical levels to find the meaning of and explanation for the societal crises of which they feel themselves part and which they want to clarify. Their examination of youth protest respects the dissenters as the subjects of societal change and accepts their demands and activities as the product of genuine probes for alternative world views. And perhaps because they see in these young intellectuals an extension of their own situation, they have usually been sympathetic, empathetic critics of their apprentice counterparts.

In the writings of McLuhan the "new culture" is presented in its most uncritical appraisal as an example of the mass media's ability to create and disseminate basic societal changes. The revolution in communications techniques, according to his thesis,[3] made possible the new generation—the first-born of the Medium-Message. Other writers, working along the same lines but delving deeper, have suggested that the causal link between changed communication techniques and the social alienation of the young set the stage for their desire to find new directions. The mass media, they point out, kaleidescopes "generations of value perspectives" so rapidly that espoused norms are continually debunked and, in most instances, instantaneously refuted and recreated by the "hard sell" pouring out of television tubes, newspapers, and song discs.[4] Brushing aside the pessimism of elitist critics of mass society, McLuhan does not see the media children as "losers," for he equates their liberation with a future already begun, and he does not find it wanting. Here again, as in the theories of postindustrial society, qualitative social change is

* For the interdisciplinary thrust, cf. e.g., departmental combinations like the Social Relations Department at Harvard, or more recently, the development of Black Studies Departments, Urban and Environmental Institutes or Schools, etc.

76

made a function of the revolution in technology, which in one way or another takes on—or is given—a life of its own.

The idea that the quantum leap in technical capabilities pierces the cultural realm finds resonance in Winthrop's suggestion that student unrest is the result of a conflict in values between industrial and postindustrial man. According to him, "The younger generation sees emerging a world of prospective automation and cybernation, of abundance and leisure, all of which make the homilies of the Protestant Ethic and the assumption of scarcity economics seem silly,"[5] and gives the current generational conflict a historically unique character. Caught in this untenable situation, youth is forced to develop new values, new horizons and new interpretations about the world. The young are of today while living in tomorrow. This is the meaning of the "now generation," and the only way to understand the gap in generational world views—which Winthrop vehemently maintains exists—is to put the differences into proper historical perspective. The youth movement, he maintains, is "real and in the vanguard of [a] transformation," therefore the social reconstruction of the values and arrangements of American society undertaken by these young people cannot be viewed as just another social problem. It is rather a product of crisis which eludes piecemeal solutions. Although Winthrop's analysis centers on the counterculture's search for alternatives on the cultural level, he avoids the psychological pitfalls of the generation-gap thesis as well as the fallacy of animated technology by pointing to the infrastructure as the primary cause of the emergence of the counterculture. He finds Parsons' suggestion that student protest is caused by incomplete or faulty socialization and therefore must be repressed inherently incorrect, for, he reasons, if the experiences of postindustrial youth are indeed new, then their trials represent the value system of a "becoming" society.

Marcuse's postulates of "cultural revolution" and "instinctual liberation," which when further developed in his later works culminated in his Marxian-derived concept of the "new man," also take off from the precondition of the changed nature of technology and the imminent arrival of an automated society. His eminence in the mid-1960's as the young people's philosopher-king is understandable in the light of their common points of departure: both took the new technology for granted and both rejected its alienating effects. In *One-Dimensional Man*, Marcuse had given primary importance to the predominance of a technocratic culture in advanced industrial societies, leading him to reject technology because it caused oppressive unidimensionality.* Many young people during this same period, especially university students who were able to pursue their studies precisely because of the "new technology," were just becoming aware of its omnipresence, and they, too, rejected its dehumanizing, 1984 qualities. The paradoxical attitude and rather diffused actions of the early student protesters seem to be related to their middle-class status, which, for the moment, obviously freed them from the immediate necessity of preparing themselves for work. Their favored situation apparently led them to the generalization that all human labor, especially in the most technically advanced countries of the world, had already been superseded by machines. As a result, many active students during the early years of the student movement took little or no notice of the continued empirical importance of work in American society, but instead adopted, as a made-to-order cloak, Marcuse's concept of the Great Refusal. Their emphasis at that time was—and for many young people still remains—the search for identity and self.

Perhaps the major criticism of Marcuse's guide to practice and early student leadership is that both were based on a myth: a possible development was believed to be a reality. A transitional period (U.S., 1964) which might eventually have led to the anticipated state (technocratic and automated society) was not seriously analyzed either in relation to the actual organization of work nor to the decision-making processes. Nor were conditions outside their immediate personal or national boundaries taken into account. For example, recognition of the importance of the relationship between the various metropoles and their dependent satellites had to wait on the insurgence of Pan-Africanism, Black Liberation, Black Power, and Latin American dependence theorists and anti-imperialist activists before the American youth movement

---

* In *One-Dimensional Man*, Marcuse takes a generally antitechnological position. Yet even in that work he is aware that advanced technical knowledge is a prerequisite for liberation.

was to overcome its rather naive pseudo-revolutionary beginnings.

Paul Goodman, like Marcuse, was a man of the Left, but his analysis took a different turn. Goodman saw the youth culture's emphasis on participatory democracy as a reaction to the bureaucratic nature of Western capitalism and Soviet socialism. But, he held, "our revolutionary situation is not a political one.... Among the young especially, the crisis is a religious one, deeper than politics. The young have ceased to 'believe' in something, and this disbelief occurs at progressively earlier years. What is at stake is not the legitimacy of American authority but any authority."[6] His interpretation* and sympathetic review, in large measure raise the same question which plagued the socialist-anarchist debate at the turn of the century: How can one build a purely antiauthoritarian countersociety within a highly structured, powerful, antagonistic, and yet seemingly flexible system without being coopted, commercialized, and thereby neutralized? The question has obviously been neither muted nor resolved. The syndicalist and anarchist strongholds in the Mediterranean exist to this day. The French student revolt of 1968 was not a minor incident. And the revival of Wobbly anarchism among American students cannot be ignored. But these temporary or probable successes pose yet another question: How does one hold on to successes once gained?

Among those social critics who maintain that the future is "new," there is a tendency to adopt a transhistorical view and to fashion a new universalism. Whether advanced in simplistic or more sophisticated tunes, their concept of the "new human being in formation" leads them to declare the emerging life-style as already existing *in nuce* and spreading. Reich again gives the best expression of this near belief.

> Consciousness III (the consciousness of liberation) has sprouted up, astonishingly and miraculously, out of the stony soil of the American Corporate State.... It is not surprising that many people think it a conspiracy, for it was spread, here and abroad, by means invisible [p. 233]....

Thus, what may be called the politics of transition—the change from the old to the new culture—is deemphasized. The layer of

* Goodman claimed that his ideas were in tune with a Kropotkin-type of anarchism.

revolutionary occurrence is seen to be only in "consciousness" and not in social structure, institutions, or modes of production, despite the passing mention of them by many of these critics.

One of the persistent worries of Marcuse is that the "new man" does not automatically appear, not even in socialist societies. Rejecting a one-sidedly materialistic approach, he, unlike Goodman and Reich, focuses on the political character and potential of consciousness and its products—art, theory, way of life—although he recognizes their mediated unity. This perspective is the crucial one for him in both capitalist and socialist societies. The continued liberation of consciousness (and with this goes the continued necessity for critical theory) is thus constitutive and indispensable for further societal and personal development. When talking specifically about Western capitalist societies, Marcuse has often pointed out the subversive potential of consciousness and theory, which, once having freed themselves from their inimical environment, start to undermine and call into question the "affirmative" culture of these societies. He argues that nonaffirmative qualities can be attributed to those nuclei of intellectuals who have started to emancipate themselves from the dehumanizing and deintellectualizing effects of the multiversity and the oppressive as well as repressive forces of society and culture.[7]

7

THE PROTEST OF
BLACK STUDENTS:
DILEMMA AND
APOLOGY

Black protest and black politics, as examples of dissent by
marginal groups, have been marked attempts to grapple and come
to terms with the effects of inequality, oppression, and exploitation
growing out of the American stratification system. Their protest in
the sixties drew on a long-standing tradition of responses to the
manipulations of ethnicity and race in different stages of American
development—a tradition that includes individual revolts, cultural
retreatism, collective rebellion, intellectual criticism, destructive
violence, and accommodation or integration reform efforts,
depending on the place accorded blacks in the economic strategies of
the particular historical moment. The mode of dissent (our list is
not complete by any means) not only reflected changing objective
conditions but also revealed the extent to which blacks have been
able to pierce the ideological distortions surrounding the American
class system. Blacks perhaps more than any other group have had to
cope with a situation in which their self-image and understanding of
their place in society are linked to a fusion of reality and apology.
Black intellectuals have been especially susceptible to such
ideological distortions, since it has been their task to create viable

visions for the ceaseless struggle of blacks to develop ways by which to enter the mainstream. The confluence of class, ethnicity, and race, and its ideological outlines, can be traced in the writings, social-scientific and other, about black protest.

In the course of this study, black students have entered our argumentation as significant examples of possible dissenters whose radical potential rests on a specific class position associated with a temporary marginality status (age) and a permanent ascribed characteristic (color). Explanations of black student protest face conceptual difficulties which may easily lead to an overemphasis of either one of these factors. Because these difficulties lie at the very cutting edge of the questions we are addressing, a critical review of the case of black students may (and we hope will) provide greater comprehension of the class system and the societal function of ascribed characteristics as both facilitators of protest and elements of economic growth.

Black student protesters are treated as part of the larger black community, and therefore social scientists do not subsume them under the simple category of student dissent. This holds true even when the central focus is on the black *student*. For a first approximation, we accept this division and present these social-scientific explanations as a separate category.

A cursory look at available analyses of white and black student protest shows some striking differences. First, black student protest in itself has been the subject of relatively few investigations, even when connected with the black movement as a whole; and second, the psychologizing approach so prevalent in studies about white students is far less frequent in studies of black student activism. Apparently researchers became persuaded early in the game that in the case of black students, personality variables alone do not provide a reliable base for predicting political actions. The few psychological studies that do exist, the most cogent of these being the one by Fishman and Solomon,[1] take off from Erikson's psychohistorical approach.

A third difference is that, unlike many of the purely behavioral and inherently ahistorical explanations of white student dissent, theories and even surveys about the political actions and attitudes of black students are infused with historical perspective. (The use of history for the most part, however, still remains anecdotal or episodic.) Consequently, the study of black student dissent generally makes it part of a continuous social movement and a manifestation of collective behavior.

Social scientists differ also in their evaluations of the two groups of protesting students. By and large these researchers, following their liberal dictates, watched white protesters sympathetically as long as they fitted into the liberal model and its implied values—that is, as long as they were serious students fighting for traditional ideals through the prescribed legal (or formal) channels. When the model of acceptable behavior appeared to be consistently abrogated, the researchers' benevolent positive neutrality vanished. Were it not for the element of race (i.e., racism), such would have also been the fate of their positive view of black student confrontation. That their attitudes did *not* change is a matter of record.

Explanations about dissenting black students divide into two categories, economic and cultural, viewed either as dichotomous or interconnected, depending at which stage of the developing protest the theories were formed.

Economic Explanations

Two different theses make up the economic mode to explain the emergence and sociopolitical significance of the sixties protest. The first locates dissent in the "status inconsistency" or "relative deprivation" of middle-class black students; the second ties it to changes in intra-black class arrangements. There is also a difference of opinion as to whether black students were the vanguard of or merely followers in the general black movement.

Early studies about the sit-ins and civil-rights activities in the South suggested that black student activity grew out of the contradiction between achieved and ascribed status.[2] In this same vein, researchers theorized that black college students felt "deprived" when comparing themselves to their white peers. In protesting, they acted out of the self-interested desire to open up occupations and positions commensurate with their education and skills. Reinterpreting newer data, one researcher found that "feelings of discontent about *personal* prospects in a bi-racial world are not associated with particularly high levels of protest and feelings about the general position of the *whole Negro* race."[3] The major conclusion drawn from the half-dozen or so studies in this early period seems to be that black students acted as concerned spokesmen for the masses of black people who, because of educational deficiencies and racial isolation, had not yet formed a consciousness of their own. Whether this conclusion was valid in its time or whether the rapidity of changes within the student movement made it well-nigh impossible to pinpoint perceptions, the vanguard role of black students appears to have been short-lived. A survey found that as early as 1962, political activism was no longer associated with socioeconomic status.[4] And by 1965 and 1966, researchers were reporting that the spread of "rising expectations" among people of long-standing impoverishment may cause them to become "dissatisfied with gradual improvement of their situation and [they may] seek to channel their energies into a social movement."[5]

These early economic explanations primarily sought the "causes" of the growing black student unrest in a correlation between socioeconomic status (occupation) and race (relative deprivation or status inconsistency). Implicit in their theoretical outline was the assumption of a status (rather than class) stratification of American society and a crude economic determinism which "regulated" this hierarchy. Their focus on "relative deprivation" tapped the racial dimension, but unfortunately the cue was overshadowed by their very simple amd vulgar economic approach that placed undue emphasis on students as mere agents, blindly reacting to objectively existing conditions. Thus, it appears, although insightfully contending that relative deprivation was a factor of poverty and race, these social scientists failed to relate it to the broader scope of the struggle and the consciousness dimension implicit in the concept.[6]

Perhaps because of their overemphasis of economic status and their concomitant reliance on census data as the principal source of information, they were blind to the possibilities of change within the movement.

What in fact occurred was a learning process which amalgamated black middle-class interests with the immediate demands of the black masses. The Kerner Commission Report of 1968[7] drew attention to the transition from an integrationist mood to a more militant consciousness and underscored the significance of the early student movement in the South as promoter of this change. In their words: "The Southern college students shook the power structure of the Negro community, made direct action temporarily preeminent as a civil-rights tactic, speeded up the process of social change in race relations, and ultimately turned the Negro protest organizations toward a deep concern with the economic and social problems of the masses" (p. 246). According to the Commission, black students occupied an important place in the Negro movement at the crucial moment when mainstream civil-rights activists, confronted with rebellion in the ghetto, were apparently dumbfounded and too inflexible to deal with the immediate needs of lower-class blacks. Students at this critical stage became leaders, synthesizers, and catalysts, guaranteeing historical continuity because their personal development and political learning processes encompassed both orientations of the sixties movement.

Writing at a later time and specifically in response to the urban riots between 1964 and 1968, the authors of the Kerner Commission Report put the earlier student protest (the sit-ins and voter registration drives) into broader historical perspective, a perspective which previous economic-oriented studies had failed to do. Later studies continued the trend. These newer interpretations placed students primarily in the role of followers. This is the view of Perkins and Higginson,[8] who tie the purely reflective nature of black student protest to the students' bourgeois position and ideology. The pseudocharacter of the black student movement as a radical or even revolutionary force, they say, is also linked to the isolation of blacks in the university and their removal from the realities of black ghetto conditions. Perkins' and Higginson's critical assessment begins with

85

the proposition that the "black freedom struggle in the United States has always been fraught with internal and external problems that are rooted in the unusual class and caste basis of American society" (p. 195). In the course of their argumentation, they adhere to a deterministic class analysis which makes for a certain theoretical ambivalence and even some internal contradictions relating primarily to what they conceive as the radical function and potential of students.[9] This ambiguity, despite an apparently clear-cut and firm theoretical perspective, seems to be an expression of their indecision about whether the black condition is a question of class or race.

Perkins and Higginson locate black revolutionary praxis in the spontaneous actions of the black masses. Although they picture black student protest as "the crucial, and perhaps necessary, link in the bourgeois revolution" (p. 221), they underscore the historically limited function of black student politics within the ongoing black liberation movement. Black students, because of their social base and class position, they suggest, will fulfill their historic mission when they comprehend the bourgeois character and historical tradition of their movement. The "ideological poverty" of the black student movement (p. 217), which we would argue to be the result of pervasive dehistoricalization affecting *all* students, black and white, according to them, manifests itself in a series of failures. Black student dissenters, Perkins and Higginson insist, have been able to develop neither a theory of society nor a realistic view of their own socioeconomic position or of their own historical and political roots. Although learning processes did occur, as the authors concede (most notably in SNCC), the student sector never transcended questions of strategy and tactics. While students may have synthesized integrationist group politics, Pan-Africanism and the search for identity, their "newly discovered black consciousness has no objective referent" (p. 197). As a result, Perkins and Higginson conclude, whether students add more ideologies and social myths, or embark on the road as critical theorists, they will never be able to pursue radical politics outside their own class and university situation nor become leaders of a black mass movement.

Perkins' and Higginson's denial of the possibility of a

86

comprehensive political learning process by "bourgeois" black students—a learning that would enable them to recognize both the interests of the "black masses" and their own as real, and on this basis transcend their class limitations—marks the deterministic, and apologetic, character of their approach. While they acknowledge that black students will enhance the emerging new professional class among blacks, they fail to see the growing subjugation of this class and the educational process under capitalist principles. A critical theory of society, if this is what Perkins and Higginson intended their analysis to be, must be totalistic and should point to the many and simultaneous processes providing the chances to learn and to comprehend. To argue that a black revolution must take account of the fundamental interests of the black masses because they are the most oppressed group in the United States does not demand the conclusion that the black masses are the *only* group within which the revolutionary potential resides.

Unlike Perkins and Higginson, Michael W. Miles attributes greater significance to the impact of cultural and intellectual traditions on the radical potential of the black student movement. In his book *The Radical Probe*,[10] he attempts to assess the origins and prospects of the movement in the context of an emerging new urban black middle class, which, especially in its liberal sectors, challenged the established black bourgeoisie. Consequently, economic and cultural explanations mesh in his analysis, which is embedded in a detailed historical description.

According to Miles, the black student movement operated as a caucus within the liberal sectors of the new black middle class. Following the leads of the liberal civil-rights movement and subsequently (in response to the social disruptions in the urban ghettoes) the nationalist and more militant orientations of the black lower classes, the protest of the black student Left helped to dismantle the institutional stronghold of the traditional bourgeoisie—its educational system. Since the black middle class, both in its traditional and modern forms, has been an essentially professional class, the students' protest against the authoritarianism of black schools, colleges, and universities, and their acquiescent subservience to the values and interests of the dominant white society, signaled a political-ideological intraclass fight. As a result, one wing of the black middle class turned toward a more race-conscious and nationalist position reminiscent of the race-radical ideas of the New Negro movement of the twenties. Student demands for the university's involvement in community-development programs and recruitment of students from lower-class backgrounds, he contends, further undermined the power of the traditional black bourgeoisie.

Miles' description and projection of the intra-middle-class rearrangements in line with liberal corporate capitalism and the emergence of nationalist movements in and outside the country seem to support the thesis that black student protesters have indeed been "the key in completing 'the bourgeois democratic revolution.' "[11] He, however, draws a different conclusion than do Perkins and Higginson. For him, the black middle-class intellectuals have been the "only consistent carriers of radical politics" (p. 244). From his projected enhancement of the black professional class and the democratization of the black educational system, there arises an interesting possibility: that there might be a greater pool of radical black intellectuals and therefore a greater potential for "radical black politics." Unfortunately, Miles fails to indicate clearly what he means by radical black politics ("nationalist self-determination, socialist revolution, or both" [p. 244]) or to specify its possible economic and political power base in American society or the international constellation of metropoles and satellites.

Cultural Explanations

The status of black Americans and other nonwhite minorities is the central social and political problem of American Society. They [blacks] began to demand access to, and participation in, all of the opportunities, rewards, benefits, and powers of America—not on the basis of race or even of citizenship, but on the basis of their very humanity. In the mid-1960s, this "bondage of the spirit" was broken, and there emerged among black students a deep and tense awareness and consciousness that a black culture existed....Black pride, Black identity, Black unity, Black power, Black self-determination, and Black survival are not idealistic notions to black students. Rather, they are fundamentally existential expressions which give meaning,

88

direction, purpose, and vitality to the contemporary black struggle.

The Report of the President's Commission on Campus Unrest[12]

The search for self-definition and cultural hubris have been major themes and a source of strength of the black movement. In the cultural hubris lie the themes of human dignity and human sameness, pride in color and race consciousness, and the currents of nationalism and Pan-Africanism, religious solace and separatism. The dialectics between themes and currents took on different forms at different times and found adherents in the different classes. But whatever the emphasis or visibility, and whatever form it took, the search circled around the principal dichotomy contained within the hubris—integration or separation.

Many interpreters of black movements in the sixties recognize or locate in the cultural hubris sources for propelling the movement, although most of them are uncomfortable about giving it overriding prominence. For this reason the cultural explanation is always circumscribed by structural referents as well as by psychohistorical elements. In this sense, it fits the holistic character of all cultural interpretations. In the case of the attempts to explain black student protest or the movement at large, the nexus is more clearly tied to the reconstruction or recounting of black history.

The cultural dimension of the civil rights movement is found primarily in the learning process or conversion of the young activists.[13] It is that historical learning process that makes them sensitive and susceptible to the experiences of the poor in urban ghettoes. And it is under the impact of riots in these ghettoes during 1964–68 that black student activists, together with black intellectuals, forged a new black consciousness and black nationalism, amalgamating the tendencies of lower-class religious nationalism with their own political experiences.

The rather rapid awakening of black consciousness and the rediscovery of black culture are considered to be the positive fallouts from the learning processes undergone by blacks in their attempts to destroy racism, and these in turn are thought to have laid the groundwork for direct confrontation. Persons studying black student confrontations after the injection of a black consciousness put greater emphasis on the cultural realm, especially as it pertains to learning. Social critic Harold Cruse[14] goes even further, asserting that the preoccupation with cultural facets of Negritude in white America should take priority over economic or political matters in the debates among black intellectuals. Cruse seems to feel that this, then, would give idea-formation a black rootedness and therefore create and at the same time rediscover a black past.

The psychocultural moratorium (the interstitial period between civil-rights agitation and black militancy) created an ambiance which allowed black writers, poets, and political critics to influence the younger generation. They helped instill in the Young Turks, both in and out of the universities and high schools, the intellectual curiosity to debate and to reconstruct a history relevant to the questions of the late sixties. Black intellectuals wrote and debated the virtues of black high culture versus folk culture and raised questions about the comparative social worth of integration and nationalism. The mounting controversy was reflected on the campus. Black students confronted their universities with demands for official recognition and curricular representation of their history and culture. They wanted and got Black Studies programs and the introduction of courses on the African and Afro-American heritage. By demanding larger college admissions quotas, they helped spread their consciousness to the public schools as well as increase the black presence on the nation's campuses.

The cultural turn of black student demands is considered relevant and important to cultural liberation (i.e., critical distance) by critics assessing the movement, and they also see the new twist as an ingredient of total liberation, but what in fact is (or ought to be) the content of "cultural liberation" leaves them divided.

For reasons common to this disagreement and because of our conviction that in the play of people making their own history lies the dialectic of the present, we set out to trace, in thematic form, those forces in the black American experience which must be considered in defining the content of liberation.

Black Intellectual Dissent: Origins and Themes[15]

The forms in which American blacks have pierced the wall of imposed exclusion and their relegation to subhuman status have been circumscribed by the use made of them in the development of capitalist enterprise in the United States. The prior existence of racial prejudice and the visible difference in color lent themselves to being turned into the major ingredients in the rationalizations for their permanent exclusion from society and the establishment of a dominant-subdominant status dichotomy. Ethnic difference was superseded by color, and while this allowed the development of parallel subcultures, color denied the indirect but active participation of blacks as a culture group in the dominant mainstream, and also denied them a direct part in the historical evolution of American society. Nonetheless, exclusion is not to be equated with noninfluence. Rather, the social relationship between master and slave has been a two-way street, even if one of the sides is a boulevard and the other an alley.

In the South, during the mercantile era, plantation owners strove for autarky, which exacerbated the provincial and geographical insularity of the plantation system. Rebellion in this social setting took the form of individual revolt against direct everyday brutality or of insurrection of a group of slaves on a single plantation. The potential of greater revolt was contained by the diversity of slave labor and the development of a hierarchical structure among blacks based on skill and type of labor (especially the difference between field and domestic work).

For blacks, status differentiation was an imposed internal development relating purely to plantation economy. For the master, status was an intraclass phenomenon which had its referent both in the Southern plantation class and external class configurations as well as in the interclass relations among Southern whites. At first, the masters' external class definition was related to the neocolonial dependence of the plantation system as a whole, and later complicated by its dependence on the emerging conditions of a capitalist set of relations. But for all of its internal contradictions (class and

91

status relations) and its external pressures (a system of slavery in an emerging capitalist society), the autarkic plantation economy lasted a long time, branding black culture with the mark of oppression.

The perceptions of American colonialists as they debated the constitutional basis of their new independence made acceptable and formalized the exclusionary precepts of Southern society—slavery. The notion that all men were created equal did not encompass blacks, nor for that matter the propertyless. The social form of the new nation was finally decided in the Civil War. Important to the black condition was the fact that slave labor was abolished in principle and capitalist forms of social relations officially instituted. The Federal government was the official agent of change in the South, and both plantation owner and slave class were intervened by this outside force. Within both strata, however, there were receptive sectors ready for change. The Abolitionist movement long before the Civil War had interjected into black-white slave relations the countermanding notion of a democratic, egalitarian social nation. But Abolitionists as well as others had not worked on pristine territory. Not all blacks were unskilled or illiterate field hands.* Some were "freedmen" who had made the big move to the city (16 percent in 1860), and some owned property.† And most Southern whites did not own slaves. An item in the pre-Civil War census of 1860 gives lie to the notion of the existence of a monolithic slave-holding white class in the South. The census found only 28 to 29 percent white Southern slave owners, and only 7 percent of the total population owning nearly three million of the almost four million slaves. The "white system" before 1865 had a large propertyless and even itinerant "mass" at the bottom.

The crisis of mid-nineteenth-century America had many ramifications. But from our specific vantage point—tracing the roots and development of black consciousness as it relates to cultural or total liberation—the resolutions of the crisis resulted in the destruction of black insularity (as well as regional dominance), permitting blacks a new and enlarged perspective with which to assess their

* Of the 10,689 freed Negroes living in New Orleans in 1860, for example, a substantial number were teachers, jewelers, architects, and lithographers. Together they owned $15 million worth of property.
† In 1860, Southern freed Negroes owned property estimated at $25 million.

previous and current status. Rising expectations (and the concrete examples of accomplished fact) of breaking their bonds and of being free nurtured the potential of group consciousness. Their dream, for the most part, was to be accepted as fully human and to be integrated.

Although the Emancipation Proclamation of 1865 recognized the crisis of a divided economy in a divided nation, it set into motion a series of contradictory but interconnected reactions rather than a resolution: the legal recognition of Negro rights circumscribed by Southern backlash and Federal withdrawal; inroads by Negroes into the social, economic, and political spheres of Southern society blocked by the resistance and violence of the Ku Klux Klan and the lynch mobs; the efforts of the newly founded Freedmen's Bureau to fulfill promises of land, jobs, and physical mobility contravened by bureaucratic stalling and finally by the dissolution of the Bureau. Nonetheless, blacks moved on several fronts. By 1900, the Negro literacy rate had risen to 42.9 percent, from 18.6 percent in 1870. A feeble but definite beginning was made in personal as well as group geographic mobility. Blacks tasted political power in the various state legislatures and began to make real but small inroads into the business and professional worlds.

As Southern reconstruction grew stronger, large numbers of blacks sought refuge in the black church, an institution which had always been largely controlled by blacks themselves. Segregationist policies had helped keep it so. Now, in a time of fresh troubles, the black church became practically the only institution to house the blacks' desire to control their religious, cultural, and social needs. Because it amalgamated the residues of rapidly rising expectations and unbearable frustration, it provided one of the principal training grounds for the growth of potential black leadership.

In periods of reaction, retreat to all-black institutions (e.g., churches) was only one aspect of a rather persistent pattern of responses by black Americans to slavery, racism, and discrimination. When disillusionment over the prospects for integration spread—as it did, for example, in the post-Revolutionary era and again, with even greater intensity, in the eighteen-fifties, after the Kansas-Nebraska Act (1854) and the Dred Scott decision (1857) seemed to have destroyed abolitionist intentions—blacks started to emphasize racial pride, solidarity, and cultural nationalism, and ventilated ideas and programs for emigration to the Caribbean and Africa.

Black nationalism, separatism, and integrationist accommodation, the roots of which lay in the eighteenth and nineteenth centuries, became the central themes of intellectual debate about which strategies and tactics would best serve to organize the black masses in the twentieth century. Black nationalist and separatist tendencies, which Martin Delaney had cogently formulated as early as 1854, draw on the specific American experiences by black people of their persisting exclusion—a crucial axis of their common cultural hubris.

Black intellectuals who saw the salvation of Negritude in separation and explored its possible direction and meaning, also tended to see the complexity of the caste-class relationship of American society. More often than not, however, they could not resolve that conflict nor provide a viable synthesis of the two orientations—separation and integration. The actions of W. E. DuBois, for example, are an example of this irresolution. Disagreeing with Booker T. Washington's policies, he formed the Niagara Movement (1905),* arguing that political activity was based (or potentially possible) on the recognition of Negritude and the importance of racial pride. In doing so, he helped concretize the separatist notion. But, as cofounder and influential member of the NAACP, he used the very concept of Negritude to fight for Negro rights, arguing that access was important for black development at that particular historical moment. In his later years, he leaned more towards the internationalist Pan-African position. The West Indian Marcus Garvey, on the other hand, organized the separatist-oriented Universal Negro Improvement Association† (which was widely accepted by the black urban lower classes), but at the same time

---

* The Niagara Movement was short-lived, but out of its trials evolved the National Association for the Advancement of Colored People, which was organized in 1910.

† Garvey founded the Association in Jamaica in 1914 but had little success with it on the island. He moved to New York in 1916 and founded the newspaper *The Negro World* and began to build his organization. His success was phenomenal. In 1919, he claimed a membership of more than two million.

bolstered the integrationist strain by supporting Negro businesses and setting up chains of grocery stores, restaurants, and even a steamship line.

World War I economic needs started pulling blacks out of the South into the Northern cities and the Great Lakes region. But even before the all-out effort of sending the Yanks "over there" (400,000 of them blacks), an official investigation by the Department of Labor in 1916 set the total migration of Negroes from the South over a period of eighteen months at 350,000. The causes given were "general dissatisfaction with conditions, the boll weevil, floods, the crop system, low wages, poor housing, poor schools, unfairness in court proceedings, and lynching.[16]

The era between the war and the Great Depression marked a new level of black experience. The rubric of the new stage took its form from the geographical movement of Southern rural blacks to the Northern and Western cities and, via the armed forces, to the outside world. As a result of wartime propaganda, the democratic mission and ethos for the first time since the Abolitionists' endeavors were inculcated anew, this time into an urban black *Gestalt* of rising expectations. But whites resisted black incursions into the tight job and housing markets and they became retaliatory and virulent. Black resistance to violence against their persons also took on new character, and they responded in a more unified and more purposeful manner. Nonetheless, old patterns learned in the South persisted. Uprooted black "peasants" created a haven in the store-front church not only as a familiar shelter but also as an acculturating device.* The urban church was an integral part of the new type of community taking shape in the larger cities throughout the United States. Whereas formerly the small number of blacks in Northern urban centers had been scattered, this era saw the emergence of black ghettoes. Encapsulation in a city ghetto symbolized a novel pattern of exclusion, and as it became more permanent (because it was *not* a port of entry into the American mainstream), it took on the character of a slum.

The effects of urbanization, the "community" of the ghetto, and the better access to the larger society, feeble though they were, made

---

* Store-front churches (Black Pentecostalism) have continually been supported and populated by the steady stream of "immigrant" blacks, especially since the mid-fifties.

for a more stable black bourgeoisie. From this mix, the urban black intellectual emerged. Between 1920 and 1930, the Harlem Renaissance Group was the expression of the potential for self-criticism in an all-black community. But for the black masses, the ghetto and urban slum conditions were the grim, everyday reminders of the new pattern of exclusion in a strange land. Garvey tapped their frustration and anger with his call for a return to black roots and his "back to Africa" movement, and the blacks rallied as they had never done before.

The Depression was a time of retrenchment and desperation for everyone. For blacks, it was even worse. What little they had gained seemed to vanish. Nonetheless, one thing was irrevocable—blacks were now firmly entrenched in the cities and the nation—and within the next twenty-five years their needs and demands would knock on the door of the highest court of the land.

World War II again set into motion the quantitative aspects of mobility—access to the occupational hierarchy—expanding the bourgeoisie, creating a skilled and semiskilled industrial-based black working class and once more the spread of greater equality. By the fifties, the qualitative consequences of these changes could be seen in two movements: the first, the well-known push for civil rights by the modern black middle class and some of the more highly skilled members of the working class; the second, the Black Muslims, principally among lower-class blacks.

Recalling th general experience of the church as "haven" (the thirties had had Father Divine) and of the smaller Muslim sect of the same period, Malcolm X drew on the urban-based exclusion, frustration, and collective anger of the poor black. In the sixties, the decade of generalized protest, the Black Muslim movement was secularized and routed into the Black Nationalist syndrome. Black students and their intellectual counterparts, when confronting white institutions and white society, were, in truth, captives of two traditions—to be black Americans or American blacks. The dichotomy was mitigated by the emergence of Third World liberation movements and the Black Panther Party. The choices of young blacks for the direction of identity were broadened and the connections between cultural liberation and total liberation made

96

clearer. Perhaps this is what is reflected in the remarks by Prathia Hall Wynn, SNCC graduate and current program director for the National Council of Negro Women, in a conversation with Marjorie Hope.

I *reject* labels like 'militant.' It is simply a question of sincere commitment. Black Power is nothing new. It's what we were after all the time. We haven't changed. I haven't changed. We are the same people who submitted our heads to the state troopers. Back in the early sixties, work in the nonviolent student movement *was* revolutionary activity, because it created a new consciousness in black people, and even some whites.

The student movement was not as the government and the press tried to paint it, an attempt to integrate into the mainstream of America. We've always known that the main-stream of American life was bloody, muddy, polluted water. James Baldwin has rightly asked, "Who wants to be integrated into a burning house?" The student movement was a revolt against the indignities America inflicted upon us as a people. It's the press and the white liberals who misinterpret our struggle. The same thing is true of the concept of Black Power. And what the administration means by Black Capitalism is a few black overseers in a position to exploit further the masses of the people.

(What you are telling me, then, is the result of your experiences of frustration.)

It's not a question of frustration! (she retorted) We are not frustrated. We recognize who the oppressor is.[17]

It should not come as any surprise, then, that the black student movement reflects the responses of black people to their condition—the strains of Pan-African Nationalism, nationalist Marxism, Black-American identity and culture, as well as bourgeois pluralistic access politics.

8

THE YOUNG ARE
THE VICTIMS

We now have the abnormal situation that, in the face of the
extraordinary novelties and complexities of modern times, there
is no persuasive program for social reconstruction, thought up
by many minds, corrected by endless criticism, made practical
by much political activity.... The young are honorable and see
the problems, but they don't know anything because we have
not taught them anything.

Paul Goodman*

Intellectuals in-the-making, the "young" and the "honorable,"
have indeed been the victims of historical and political disconti-
nuity. They themselves have attested to it both in words and in
action. This disruption has been abetted by an intellectual climate
marked by technocratic apologies. Belated and largely ahistorical
Marxian as well as other types of critical analyses have not cleared
the muddy waters. But to say, as Goodman does, that the "older"
generation did not "know" and therefore did not "teach," is open to
question.

Having come to the end of the first part of our *Ideologiekritik*, it is
advisable to pause briefly and review the essential characteristics of
this climate partly created, and certainly advanced, by social
scientists who dealt with the problems attendent to student unrest.
We cannot fully assess their impact at this point, but we can state
that the social-scientific theories during the sixties explored issues

* Remarks to a group of university students, 1971.

either in direct contrast to or at sharp variance with the initial probing of students into the meaning of their habitat. From the very outset, the academic ambience seems to have inhibited any recognition of the justice of student criticisms. While students were following their bent, which seemed to be pushing them ever closer to challenging the "system," most of their mentors continued unperturbedly to spin their theories within the parameters of the *status quo*, apparently accepting these as the only frame of reference for their scientific discourse. It is not at all surprising, therefore, that given their pedantic adherence to the results of their own political and professional socialization, the teachers could no longer serve as mentors to the young. When confronted with student unrest, they used their ready-made schemes to find logical "reasons" for the outbursts. And they "justifiably" could lend their sympathies. But when faced with persistent denials of their suggested solutions to the problems and firm refusal to use the method of democratic persuasion, their sympathies waned. No longer able to justify defiance of the market-place mechanism of the "good society," they became aggressive apologists. In retrospect, their short-lived sympathies seem to have flowed from their own life histories and the general liberalism which flowered on most college campuses in the euphoria of finally being freed from the stifling overcautiousness imposed by McCarthyism, which, at first abetted by academic cold warriors, in the end boomeranged and took on the eggheads themselves.

A number of the social scientists whose work we have reviewed took part in the ideological debates of the Depression years over possible societal directions and alternative roads. They were then the Young Turks, anxious, ready, better-schooled than most, and hard-hit by the realities of economic disaster. This participation, in turn, permitted them to appear (and perhaps to believe) to be historically "rooted" and conscious, while through their theories they acted as agents of the dehistoricization process characteristic of the fifties and sixties. Thus they became active purveyors and preparers of the conditions which allowed the development of a full-blown technocratic culture. Although in their theoretical explorations and empirical methods—that is, in their academic

100

activities—they have displayed complex knowledge and technical expertise, they have, willy-nilly, served as legitimators and ideologues of a societal development which they apparently deem good, necessary, and natural.

Neomarxist theorists in good Hegelian fashion belatedly included students among the possible agents for bringing about qualitative change. Their projections of peripheral groups (marginals) and the "new working class" (students and intellectuals) as potential revolutionaries, however, have not been sufficiently complemented by an exploration of the specific historical development of American society nor of the immediate context within which protest occurred. Perhaps their projections, however antithetical to their adversaries, are similarly twisted by an ideology which makes the "uniqueness" of America's ethnic stratification more important than the basic class structure of the whole of American society. This, at least, is our contention. Since this chapter is neither summary nor transition, we shall anticipate one of the points we make in the concluding chapter in support of our contention. If the possible agents of change in the United States can be pinpointed, it lies in the specific development of productive forces that do not "create" marginals but instead boldly make visible prior existing marginals and the ever-increasing number of persons capable of understanding their "alienated" position—an attentive and disposable group, made malleable by the promise of future usability (gratification) and temporarily content by creature comfort satisfaction (consumerism).

At first sight, Neomarxists may seem to exhibit the qualities which place them in our category of critical intellectuals. However, this is not necessarily so. There is the real danger that if they continue to employ their categories mechanically (that is, ahistorically), they will also tend to produce social mystifications and thereby countermand their critical faculty.[1] There is no question, for example, that so-called Left *tecnicós* are alive and doing well here in the United States as well as abroad.

Our typology of the theories concerning protest phenomena has illuminated the import of historical and critical elements in the scientific process. Once having chosen to join the scholarly discourse itself and to follow its development, we could not help but recognize the growing division between technocratically and intellectually oriented arguments in the academic debate about student protest and their demands for change. The use of the typology has revealed the various shades of technocratic and intellectual inclinations among the academics. Our *Ideologiekritik*, does not end with these cursory and partial conclusions. On the contrary, the ideological bent of these theories will be put into more adequate perspective in the next section, in which they are complemented with a historical sketch of the important changes in American society, the institutional and cultural adjustments thereto, and the accompanying dissonances among the social classes which have come into play with their development.

Two warnings should accompany the reading of the following section. First, it is *not* an in-depth analysis of the economic structure and development of capitalism in the United States. Rather, it is directed at the way in which Americans perceive themselves, how they are affected by this perception, and how they arrived at it. Nonetheless, an analysis of the development of both self-perception and capitalism is implicitly carried through in our overview. For example, the swift change from a mercantile to a capitalist marketplace before the nineteenth century, and the growing corporate nature of capitalism, which came to full fruition in the thirties and forties, are clearly taken into account.

The second warning concerns the connection between our typology of explanations of student protest and their roots in American history. The types are not specifically linked to individual historical events or constellations, for we are of the opinion that one-to-one causal connections are false, since they do not exist except in the imagination of those who would order the universe of happenings by the simple imposition of categories.

One other matter needs forewarning. Since "history" is not being rewritten in the following pages, we have elected to draw certain over-all trends from pre–twentieth-century America and to focus more specifically on events after 1920.

9

TAPESTRY AND SETTING: A SOCIOHISTORICAL REVIEW OF CHANGES IN AMERICAN SOCIETY

The United States may properly claim the title of the first new nation. It was the first major colony successfully to break away from colonial rule through revolution.

The First New Nation
SEYMOUR M. LIPSET

I

The factual and fictional ingredients of the American everyman's view of his country's beginnings and national history are again invoked in Lipset's thesis. The spirit of colonial revolutionary fervor as the sole progenitor of the "new" nation, in his view, takes on a

103

fictional cast by its isolation from the usurpation of Indian lands, wealth, and peoples by the early colonizers—usurpations facilitated by decentralized and widely separated Indian nations, permitting a geographic and power vacuum to become the handmaiden of colonial expansionism. It is from this dissociation that the myth of the purely anticolonial origin of the American nation springs, allowing a distorted reality to develop for most Americans, and, lamentably, also for their social scientists. Perhaps it is just because the colonists were successful in two opposing spheres—their victorious rebellion in the name of Enlightenment precepts and the continuous victories of their own imperial colonization—that the fulfillment of the democratic promise of colonial revolt has remained a nagging moral issue in American politics.

Important changes certainly were initiated by colonial separation from England, laying the basis for a greater economic and social equality and a broader political participation in the newly founded nation than previously known in the Western world. But, "fact" also resides in remembering that these proclaimed changes, which became the essence of the spirit of 1776, were propositions offered by an enlightened segment of a propertied class faced by the necessity of creating and defending its newly acquired position. Thus at the very least, contrary to the common view, the American Revolution and antecedent colonial activities brought with them two traditions: a democratic enthusiasm for equality inspired by the ideas of the Enlightenment, and the inequality forced by a reaffirmation of the primacy of individual property rights necessitated by emergent capitalist production. Both traditions were consecrated in the revolutionary zeal brought to an intraclass struggle by persons who, although living on opposite sides of the Atlantic, were of the same social and economic backgrounds and shared the same interests. The full equality of the democratic promise, however, has yet to be fulfilled and its ethical unity achieved. The most recent manifestation of the dilemma this poses is in the student and black protests of the sixties, its earliest stigmata having been in taxpayers' revolts and the schizophrenia of Jacksonianism—equality for the frontiersman and expulsion and death for the Indian.

These contradictory and interlaced tendencies, buttressed by

104

selective factual and fictional descriptions of the country's beginnings, have been expressed in different forms throughout its history and have contributed to a democratic life-style called the "American Way." The anticolonial aspect has become part of the democratic myth which has initiated many emancipatory processes both within and without the country, among them, for example, the popular push for access of previously excluded groups—the propertyless and the ethnic and racial minorities—and the well-known American predilection for backing the underdog. The colonialism aspect, on the other hand, inspired the frontier movement, the Monroe Doctrine and, in more recent time, the pretense to world leadership.

There is also no doubt that the new American nation was favored. Its enormous natural wealth, its geography, and its ability to take refuge in isolation in times of stress and rapid economic growth allowed for the containment of its two contradictory traditions. It is only recently that this country has become increasingly unable to manage and continue to obscure the empirically irreconcilable currents of its cultural and political traditions. The Vietnam war—the international expression of an imperialism imbued with democratic mission—and the protest movements of the sixties at home have tied together the foreign and domestic aspects of this contradiction, making it ever more manifest and, seemingly, making its former escape hatches obsolete.

Tied to the interplay of the two countervailing strains in America's beginnings—imperial colonialism and democratic ethos—is the evolution of the American character and its self-image, which mold the way Americans define their democratic way of life. Certainly it will be remembered that witches were burned in Salem and other Puritan communities by the very people who loudly proclaimed their belief in freedom and democracy. As has often been pointed out, most of the early immigrants, including those of wealth, came to this continent for particular redresses. The religious dissenters, debtors, prisoners, adventurers, and mavericks who could not find their niche in European society sought specific freedoms which they lacked and for which they suffered persecution and deprivation in the old world. Coming in small, cohesive groups they sought free expression for their dissenting views through tightly knit and disciplined group effort. This common form of expedient action laid the basis for an accommodation among them that emphasized the value of group identification and protection without destroying the singularity of their purpose—the right to pursue their individual lives as they saw fit.

Although these immigrants carried the Enlightenment's democratic ethos which grew out of eighteenth- and nineteenth-century European ideas about human nature, contractual relations between free individuals, the forms of democratic governments, and the nature of human fulfillment and happiness, most of them were not the groups most actively engaged in the formulation and modification of and debates about these ideas and ideals. Rather, they saw themselves as the victims of the political and personal power struggles between urban-based intellectuals and politicians, the visible protagonists of these debates, and it was to them that they attributed their distress. Nor was the physical roughness of the new continent conducive to changing their anti-intellectual and anti-urban attitudes. Instead, the necessity for coping with the immediate practical problems of survival, together with active withdrawal from their native lands in search of a place where they would have the right to pursue their beliefs, strengthened their predisposition toward idiosyncratic individual behavior—a trait generally considered singularly typical of the American character.

Along with this strong pragmatism and utilitarianism there developed a small nucleus of intellectuals who brought a historical consciousness to the new world, creating new syntheses of European and American culture and laying the foundations for a native revolutionary intellectual tradition. Thus Benjamin Franklin, for all his lowly beginnings and practical concerns, was lionized by the intellectuals of the French salons while serving as the new-nation's first ambassador to the Court of Louis XVI. He translated and transmitted to Americans the latest turns in the ongoing debate on democratic government, and at the same time acquainted the French with the American variant. Thomas Jefferson, elitist and individualistic though he was, committed himself to the ideas of a truly democratic, knowledgeable agricultural society, and firmly

106

wrote into the Declaration of Independence his belief in the possibility of such a society as well as the revolutionary concept of the people's right "to alter or abolish" the governments they created. Radical dissenters (of whom Thomas Paine was one) concerned with restoring a religious conscience to the center of American experience also played their part in the radical revolutionary movement. By synthesizing the secular and sacred, by connecting Rousseau, Locke, and "Christian liberties," they tied Christian conscience to natural law and rights, giving existential meaning to the "inalienable right" to revolution. Thus Paine was able to propound that the American Revolution was "a revolution in the principles and practice of government" and not "merely a separation from England."*

Nonetheless, these New World intellectuals and immigrant groups colonized the new continent in the same spirit: a burgeoning capitalist ethic promoting the colonial powers of the era. The spirit of capitalism became the common cultural matrix of the new Americans and inspired the liberal utopia of the new nation. Shared experiences of the "revolutionary" era together with the colonists' relatively similar cultural heritage—language, religious orientation, and ethic—were to give further impetus and common cause to the creation of a new society. Although these early immigrant groups remained true to fighting the forces of their own, limited persecution, their efforts remained mere variations of this common spirit.

Democratic intentions, however, were not fully challenged until the late nineteenth and twentieth centuries, with the massive influx of "new" immigrants. The newcomers came from different cultural backgrounds and geographic regions, bringing with them their own ideas about freedom and equality as well as the firm belief that their dreams could be realized in America. Their challenge resulted in the concept of the "melting pot," which reflects both an honest hope and an expressed necessity to remake the newcomers into white, Anglo-Saxon Americans so that the underlying homogeneity of the population and the common cultural matrix could be maintained and continued.

* "Rights of Man, Part Second," in Philip Foner (ed.), *The Complete Writings of Thomas Paine* (New York: 1945), I, 354, as quoted by Staughton Lynd, *Intellectual Origins of American Radicalism*, Introduction, p. 3.

An important part of the American myth stemming from the democratic ethos was the notion of equality which harbored, however unspoken, the dream of a classless society. Education was the leaven through which individuals were to be made mobile and fully participating citizens of a libertarian society. Rapid economic growth and the development of the frontier after the Civil War gave reality to these hopes for individual social mobility, blurring class distinctions and nourishing the possibility of a utopia of equality. But if class was blurred, group differences were highlighted. Although most immigrants were poor, their poverty was perceived, by themselves as well as others, as transitory. Part of their acculturation of becoming an American was the reinforcement of their belief in individual mobility and in the openness of American society. But this was tempered with the tacit societal recognition of group differences, allowing new immigrants the comfort of a continued cultural identity in terms of their religion and the transmission of certain Old World traditions. The American character was thus reinforced and forged anew, made up of amalgamation into the melting pot on the one hand, and the possibility, even the necessity, of subcultural or group affiliation on the other. The seeming harmony of these processes was reinforced by the boot-strap lore extolling individual success. From these stories, real and embellished, the Horatio Alger myth was born. Status seeking, deferred gratification, material symbols of "making it," and middle-classism comprised the set of values which was to become both myth and reality in twentieth-century America. And it was in this way that the democratic ethos was to take on the cloak of consumerism.

Puritan practicality and liberal utilitarianism provided the rationale for keeping the strains between social class, mobility, and new scientific and technical demands in balance during the second industrial revolution. Education was again viewed as the leavening device which could coordinate the requirements of economic growth with the American dream of equality and liberty. Not only was the number of secondary schools increased and their curricula broadened to include updated vocational skills, but American higher education was opened up to the "democratic will." In 1862,

Congress, by passing the Morrill Act, gave both monies and land for the establishment of at least one college in each of the states in support of "such branches of learning as are related to agriculture and the mechanical arts . . . in order to promote the liberal and practical education of the industrial classes in the several pursuits and professions in life." From about 1880, the American university began to show visible signs of following in close order the organizational structure and purposes of the new industrialism: as industry experimented with new productive methods and techniques, so did the university; as industry changed its leadership from the robber baron entrepreneur to the more palatable executive type, so did the university. By 1910, after a period of about twenty years of experimentation and curriculum revision, the major characteristics of the modern American university had gelled. The executive function was taken over by the "new professionals," and the administration became a powerful third force in the university. In 1906, the faculty, faced with the growing size and impersonalism of the university as well as the compartmentalization of the disciplines due to growing scientific specialization, organized the American Association of University Professors (AAUP) in order to gain some measure of protection. Students, being a larger group, were increasingly subjected to the impersonal processing of selection procedures and counseling based on psychological testing devices, while their social life continued to be controlled by university officials acting *in loco parentis*. In the newly established graduate centers, further socialization took the form of professionalism. Thus, although educational opportunities during this period of industrial expansion and large immigration were extended to many more persons than ever before, expansion was accomplished by changing the unspoken democratic principle of possible "mobility for all" into the reasonable and justifiable "mobility for some." That is, the underlying rationale of individual mobility was now, more than ever, to depend on educational credentials based on the objective criteria of merit selection and professionalism by scholarship.

From the earliest beginnings of the American nation, however, there have always been large groups that were excluded from the polity and the predominant culture. The most numerous, important, and morally inexplicable (that is, inexplicable in terms of American ideals) of course, are the blacks. After the United States became more fully industrialized, especially after the eighteen-seventies and eighties, the laboring class as a whole was, next to the blacks, the largest single group to become the subject of explicit exclusion. Through a long and not always uphill application of collective effort and group solidarity, and despite violent and bloody reaction, workers were the first such group to succeed in gaining some measure of power over their lives and defining their rights.* Their victories dealt the first serious blow to the established belief in strict individualism, but the value of individual mobility was not thereby destroyed. Rather, as was argued by the architects of the New Deal, the recognition of these collective rights was specifically meant to redress the powerlessness of the individual in the new industrial society who was faced by the necessarily increased size and power of corporate organizations' hold on the economic and labor markets. The intention was to permit individual workers, backed by group (union) support, to be free again to act on their own behalf in the economic marketplace and divert them from organizing politically. Since then, the belief in individual mobility has been subjected to a continuous series of blows. The organization of large-scale industry, the Depression of the thirties, the state of war since 1940, as well as the more recent displacement of on-the-job training by highly specialized and long-term education have changed the avenues of individual mobility and have set in motion a search for new alternatives.

Depoliticization—the separation of values, of Weltanschauungen, of ideals from "choice," of ways to act and think—helped mold the numerous group differences into the common culture of the new industrial state. It erased all concepts of utopian goals, of basic differences in vision around which public debate could take place. It assumed commonly accepted parameters of societal possibilities and prevented a debate of alternatives. *Priorities* rather than *alternatives* became the order of the day. The victory of Samuel Gompers' idea that economic unionism should become the dominant mode of labor organization was, in fact, the first grand separation of institutional

* Formal legitimacy came with the passage of the Wagner Act in 1935, which established the National Labor Relations Board.

spheres of action and the elimination of political criteria from general modes of thought. The victory served to focus the attention of the growing working population at the turn of the century on the everyday necessities of working conditions and wages.

But if individualism was subjected to reinterpretation, it gathered strength from the very consequences of its redefinition. Protected individual mobility gained had its corollary in the reinforced assumption that the citizenry would recognize the necessity of separate modes of means—ends behavior in differentiated institutional spheres. For example, persons were to comport themselves according to one set of precepts in matters of religion, and according to another in business, and so on. The major consequence of the reemphasis on individual rights (now narrowed but safeguarded) was the increasing depoliticization of the American public—a process which more than any other prepared the way for further encroachments on the democratic desires of the people.

Substituted for politics in the grand sense of competing ideas about ways to organize the social polity was the play of interest groups, variously defined as voluntary associations or political parties, or ethnic and minority subcultures. *Politicking* as a means of satisfying needs and desires, of bargaining for necessities from seemingly scarce resources, became the rule of the game. Politics was privatized, ideological debate was left to intellectual "freaks," and the unique American phenomenon of the political ward boss and political machine controlled "the game," drawing its power from the "fix," and the bestowal of "favors." Another uniquely American perception rests on the questionable victory of workers to organize only along economic lines. Socialism (Marxism), because it demanded political discourse contradicted the assumption of differentiated spheres of everyday life, was pronounced "alien" to the American way. The recurring Red scares, beginning with the Haymarket Massacre, found their legitimating consensus in this "common" cultural agreement. It was not until the surfacing of Black Power, however, that a *political* group consciousness developed on a larger scale.* And even then, the concern for group access was

* This emphasis is not meant to belittle the efforts or intent of such unions as the IWW or the political arm of the CIO, nor does it ignore the various parties and organizations of the Left. Nonetheless, the fact remains that none of these movements managed to get the same mass

coupled with the issues of group or individual identity. Today the uneasy marriage between group consciousness and individualism casts doubt on the widespread existence of a truly political group consciousness, even among blacks and other allegedly politicized groups which took part in the theater of public protest in the sixties.

Since the end of World War II, the contradiction between imperial colonialism and democratic ethos has been overlaid by a growing trend toward a technocratic culture, reflecting the technical modifications in the spheres of production and distribution of an otherwise fundamentally unchanged economic system. Anti-intellectual sentiment, still a dominant characteristic of the American public has aided and abetted the spread of this new culture, which carries in its wake a dehistoricization as well as a perversion of the democratic ethos.

Important to the evolving definition of this new culture is the manner in which it handles the legacy of debate on the relationship between progress and equality. The Declaration of Independence and the Constitution had formalized the state of the eighteenth-century debate about democracy, tying the idea of progress to human fulfillment and greater equality in the New World. In the next century, as mercantilism gave way to a full-fledged capitalist system, the notion of progress was infused with utilitarian elements, and equality was hedged in by the mundane concept of usefulness. Technocratic interpretations of progress have again redefined the idea of human fulfillment, this time as "expediency," "efficiency," "sustained economic growth," and "scientific-technical progress," going much beyond the utilitarian conceptualization and perhaps pushing it to unintended extremes. "Progress" in the technocratic culture is becoming stylized into "technical advances" whose historical basis, parameters and ends are being progressively eliminated from memory. Technocratic consciousness, however, in our opinion has not yet become an all-pervasive or predominant cultural mode, and it is not at all certain that the current trend will continue to block the possible development of a historically enlightened and humanistic modern culture befitting a technically highly developed society. It is because of this persuasion that we
support (or even massive positive sanctioning) as did the blacks in the latter part of the sixties.

have undertaken the task not only of reexamining the meaning of the protest movement with regard to systemic changes, but also to review the explanations given by intellectuals and social scientists about the continuing state of inequality among the various social classes. True, critical intellectuals generally find themselves in opposition to technocrats, whether these technocrats be apologists or specialists. The debate over the principles of equality, liberty, and freedom, however, lies in the province of the ongoing debates between apologists and critics. The antagonism has very special overtones, since intellectuals and technocratic apologists generally have similar education, training, humanistic backgrounds and at times even use similar terminology although with semantic differences. They disagree, for example, most profoundly about the proper approach to social policies, the ought-function of the modern university, and the direction the American democracy should take. The issues raised by the students in the sixties and the ensuing intellectual and political controversies served to bring into sharp relief the growing differences between technocrats and intellectuals, both within and without the universities.

In previous chapters we have examined the extent to which the social scientists are affected by the technocratic culture and the difficulties they have in adjudicating between the demands of their overt ethics and their sometimes unconscious conversion to the idea of a "postindustrial" technological society. One might say that many of them, willingly or not, have served successfully as agents of this new consciousness. The fact that most of the early student protesters when they began to voice their grievances had no theoretical referents and knew little about their historical roots is but another indication of the widespread ahistoricism of this era. What then, given these handicaps, has been the basis of the intellectual strength of the protest movement of the sixties? The answer appears to lie in the fact that a mere handful of dissident-prone students and intellectuals were able to tap the still viable, though dormant, democratic ethos of a sufficient number of others, students and nonstudents, blacks and whites, to plunge the universities and the country into deep crisis. This nucleus of intellectuals among the younger generation seems to have been the

113

recipients of a political heritage transmitted to them ·by their parents and McCarthyized but not completely silenced dissenters who had taken part in radical activities in the twenties, thirties, and the antifascist war of the forties. This intrafamily and intragroup political socialization, as far as we can ascertain, occurred through the transmission of cultural and political values and general perspectives of Weltanschauungen rather than formal instruction in specific political doctrines.* We suggest that this socialization furnished the earlier activist students with the potential predisposition for an almost instantaneous insight into the contradictory relations between their educational choices and the misuses of education, reason, and rationality in the larger society. In short, they were a "readied" group who *felt* rather than *knew* the consequences of what they perceived as the newest and latest attack on the American democratic ethos.

II

The twenties in the United States were epitomized by the "lost generation"—the incarnation of disequilibrium and escapism—and anti-Bolshevism. Post-World War I economy had intensified the uneven development between the explosive surge of industrial production and paper wealth of the late nineteenth and early twentieth centuries. The economy of normalcy culminated in the stock-market crash of 1929. World War I, among other things an expression of international economic competition, had created a situation in which capitalism not only was plunged into an almost fatal global economic crisis, but, with the success of the Russian Bolshevik Revolution in 1917, for the first time found itself seriously challenged by an alternative economic and poltical system. Some European countries, especially those with a socialist tradition, witnessed revolutionary attempts to establish this alternative within their own borders. In the United States, an anti-Bolshevik campaign was begun in anticipation of possible threats of similar internal

* For some hint of the empirical efficacy (i.e., survey results) of this suggestion, *see* esp. Seymour M. Lipset and Philip G. Altbach's critical essay on "Student Politics and Higher Education in the United States," in S. M. Lipset (ed.), *Student Politics* (New York: Basic Books, 1967), pp. 199–252.

uprisings. In addition to sending token American expeditionary forces in 1921 to help overthrow the Bolshevik regime, internal reaction sought to protect the nation by attacking the small, scattered anarchist, syndicalist, and socialist groups already disorganized by internal ideological quarrels spawned by the formation of the Communist Third International.

Attempts to organize a movement to protest the effects of postwar economic and social disequilibrium were by and large contained by the Red scare.* Nonetheless, the twenties were still a period of limited but intensive union activity. One such pocket was among the new Jewish East-European immigrants who had brought with them a utopian socialism and had found their place in the growing garment industry and other secondary industrial enterprises on the eastern seaboard. Another was among the Wobblis, members of a socialist-anarchist union (IWW), which drew on both socialist philosophy and traditional American idiosyncratic individualism. The IWW gained strength, only to lose it by 1929,† leaving isolated vestiges in the great Northwest, a legacy of workers' songs and literature, and a latent indigenous resource for future radicals. But for pursued and pursuer, the anticommunist campaign of the twenties crystallized with the murder frame-up of two immigrant Italian anarchists living in Boston—Nicola Sacco and Bartolomeo Vanzetti, the first a fisherman and the second, a shoemaker, both dedicated radical unionists.‡ Much of the political education and organizational energies of the Left and left-leaning groups were

* The passage of the Espionage Act on June 15, 1917, is frequently held to spell the beginning of the red witch-hunt. The very next day, the *American Socialist* was banned from the mails. By July, 1,200 striking Wobblies were corralled in a ball park in Bisbee, Arizona. In the early 1920s, during the infamous Palmer Raids, 10,000 so-called Communists and Communist sympathizers were arrested. Habeas corpus was suspended for many of them, and union members feared for their lives.

† Although the Industrial Workers of the World (IWW) was not founded until 1905, the high point of anarchist activity in the United States (mostly west of the Mississippi) was during the 1870s and 1880s. It was four anarchists who were executed for their alleged connection with a bomb-throwing incident which started the Haymarket Riots in Chicago on May 4, 1886. The wife of one of them, Lucy Parsons, was one of the organizers of the IWW.

‡ Sacco and Vanzetti were accused and found guilty of murdering F. A. Parmenter, paymaster of a shoe factory, and Alessandro Berardelli, a guard in South Braintree, Mass., on April 15, 1920. An independent investigatory committee consisting of President A. Lawrence Lowell of Harvard University, President Samuel W. Stratton of the Massachusetts Institute of Technology, and Robert Grant, a former judge, agreed with the governor's decision to deny clemency, despite persuasive evidence of their innocence.

derived from as well as organized around their defense. Between 1922 and 1927 (the year of their execution), native-born left-wing dissidents and European immigrants of the Left forged a common bond and, however harried and made outcast, protest sentiment joined with the democratic tradition to become a more sophisticated and acceptable stance in American politics. The anticommunist campaign served another major purpose: the harassment and containment of the labor movement. The year 1924 saw the American Federation of Labor's membership at its lowest ebb—retribution was visited on Gompers' middle-of-the-road economic unionists, although they too had joined in the Palmer Raids man-hunts.

The countervailing theme in the twenties to this basically working-class protest movement and its socialist-anarchist overtones was the escapism exhibited by the more well-to-do sectors of American society. Escapism sought refuge in being "wet," the not-too-clandestine speakeasy, bath-tub gin, the flight of many intellectuals (small group though they were) to Europe, and a glorious spirit of a wanton spending of time, talent, and money. The Jazz Age, as F. Scott Fitzgerald, one of the twenties major novelists said, had no interest in politics at all. There was, among these children of the first lost generation, a feeling of despair, shared by many men in public office who were also disillusioned by the failure of the Yanks who had gone "over there" to fulfill the American Dream of a democratic world rebuilt in the image of the new nation. In the midst of this display of disenchantment and romantic retreatism, a black renaissance was taking place among black intellectuals in Harlem and Greenwich Village. These groups, which had been meeting and gathering strength since the turn of the century, were addressing themselves to the question of the emancipation and liberation of their people. Prominent black artists, musicians, and writers were engaging in political and intellectual debate on the Marcus Garvey "Back-to-Africa" Movement, on the relationship of black radicals to the American radical Left and Communist parties, on the defintion of an ethnic politics, as well as on the relationship between black intellectuals and the black masses.

The stock market crash of 1929 signaled the collapse of an unbalanced economy and ushered in a decade of world-wide depression. In the United States, the citizenry responded by electing New York's Democratic Governor, Franklin Delano Roosevelt, a liberal aristocrat well-versed in American ward politics, to the Presidency. He immediately started (some say by sheer intuition) to reorganize the crisis-ridden economy. With his famous "Alphabet Soup" set of recovery programs,* he ushered in welfare capitalism, giving new strength and increased flexibility to the faltering economic system. With the New Deal, social engineering, spearheaded by the concerned and eager men of F.D.R.'s kitchen cabinet, came into its own. Under his political guidance, economists, political analysts, and administrators suggested and made policy for the businessmen and industrialists who had set themselves the self-interested task of patching up the disequilibrated exchange system. The social engineers of the thirties did not find this task inimical. For the most part, their approach took off from a liberal and humanistic tradition. They believed that a democratic liberal society could be sustained within the boundaries of capitalism. Their approach is not to be confused with the elitist and corporativist technocratic political movement begun in the twenties, which sought a scientifically managed and controlled society. Nonetheless, the social engineers of the New Deal and these technocrats shared a noncritical acceptance of the principles of the system itself.

Despite long breadlines, massive unemployment, and business failures, there was a sense among Americans that their economic plight was attributable not to individual failure, but rather to a diffuse and generalized malaise, a feeling reinforced by the federal policies emanating from Washington. Although massive discontent existed and formal protest was organized by both the Left and Right, on the whole, massive disruptive potentials were contained by a pervasive sense of helplessness which translated itself into a feeling of community. A common bond seemed to weave the country together, readying the American community for the directions and remedies of the New Deal.

* The "Alphabet Soup" included the NRA (National Recovery Act), WPA (Works Projects Administration), TVA (Tennessee Valley Authority), NLRB (National Labor Relations Board) as well as various regulatory agencies.

117

Nurtured by economic crisis, radical protest strengthened the tenuous foothold of legitimacy it had gained the decade before. It organized more people and affected more social groups than ever before. It was, however, never to reach mass proportions, although its potential was viewed as sufficiently dangerous to set into motion one of the most virulent counterattacks—again in the name of anticommunism—the United States had yet experienced. Dissent on the Left had spread on three main fronts: in the labor movement, among intellectuals and students, and, by their collaboration, on the political front. By 1936, the stolidly conservative American Federation of Labor was challenged by the Congress of Industrial Organizations (CIO). The new organization, in keeping with changed production techniques and growing worker unrest, broke with two American union traditions: it organized workers vertically in the mass-production industries, and it provided for the political expression of working-class economic and social needs through a political arm, the Political Action Committee (PAC). PAC, in its short life, educated and helped to coalesce working-class opinion and was highly effective as a political action group in local elections in 1942 and even more so in the national elections of 1944. The attempt to politicize the labor movement, however, was to fail. By 1948, PAC had been disbanded, and the CIO, after having first rid itself of most of its so-called Communist leadership, reaffiliated with the now more conciliatory and liberalized AFL. If the purpose of the New Deal and its creator, President Roosevelt, was not only to set in motion the necessary corrective measures to rebalance the economy but also to reorder the power relations between the various social classes in recognition of America's transformation into a national industrial state, then one of his greatest successes was the final resting place of organized labor. The New Deal had pumped into labor sufficient power (through federal support and recognition of their right to organize) so that it would act and view itself as a vested national interest group rather than a class-based movement.

Among the literati, Thomas Wolfe became the symbol of personal exploration and final social rejection of the escapist intellectual of the twenties, and Ernest Hemingway found himself in the new novel of strength and the search for relief from social alienation. Writers and poets recognized an urban America, its problems and promises. They turned from the muckraking exposure of urban and industrial ills to an examination of the causes for the maldistribution of wealth and the good life. Their angry voices created the realism of the Federal Theater Project and spurred the art of the modern dance, the stage saw the personal pangs of utopian yearnings explored in "Squaring the Circle" and "Waiting for Lefty," and even the success of the garment workers' musical "Pins and Needles." The pervasive feelings of national community, of common plight and common misgivings, brought a renaissance of critical review: John Steinbeck's *Grapes of Wrath* (1939), Carl Sandburg's *The People, Yes* (1936), Ernest Hemingway's *To Have and Have Not* (1937), John Dos Passos *U.S.A.* trilogy (*42nd Parallel*, 1930; *1919*, 1932; and *The Big Money*, 1936), and a host of others. Negro artists and intellectuals founded a new journal, *New Challenge* (1934–37), featuring the writings of Langston Hughes, James Weldon Johnson, Frank Yerby, Ralph Ellison, and William Attaway among many others.

Left dissidence turned from an anarchist and syndicalist direction to that of scientific socialism: education and action became the new slogans. By the mid-thirties, liberals had joined with the Left to form a "United Front." Despite the many differences within this loose coalition, the growing threat of Fascism and Nazism, the malfunctioning economy, and the Spanish Civil War provided acceptable grounds upon which to take collective political actions. Together they fought for labor's right to collective bargaining and organization, for full social security and public social services, opposed the President's economic embargo against the Spanish democratic government, and opposed war and Fascism. On the college campuses, students founded the American Student Union and later the American Youth Congress, the first nationwide voices of organized student protest.

But the return to full engagement with the democratic ethos—which to left-wing dissenters of the thirties meant the broadening and securing of equality, peace, and antitotalitarianism—produced not only political and intellectual euphoria, but also intense disagreements over the ways and means of implementing their desired goals. The 1939 German-Russian

Mutual Assistance Pact came as a shock to most of the Western world for many reasons, not all of which due to the higher morality of a better world order. For the Left and its sympathizers it laid bare the tenuous ties of coalition, causing the fragile cup of "popular unity" to shatter into personal vindictiveness, social-psychological inefficacy, and political bankruptcy. For students, the future generations of intellectuals, the pact meant a damning interjection of *Realpolitik* into their ahistorical and highly academic utopias. We cannot explore their specific traumas in this necessarily schematic overview. What is important, however, is to note the concrete trajectory of their behavior as a result of the pact's effect on their political socialization. Most of these young people threw themselves into the "fighting" war against Nazism, and many were to turn into cold warriors. At least to those who still thought of themselves as liberals or democratic Leftists, their assistance in the destruction of the Communist Left (which they did with great fervor) seemed the psychotherapy of a shattered youthful idealism. In the case of the future social scientists (and many were to reach the top of the establishment), at least twenty years passed before their 1939 trauma manifested itself explicitly. This they did by elaborating an explanatory model of modern society which proclaimed the end of ideologies, raised democratic pluralism to utopian levels, and heralded the millennium of technomeritocracy.

As the Left grew because of economic crisis, so did the Right. Right protest manifested itself in the Black Shirts (a small group of young people whose nationalism was stirred by Mussolini) and the Brown Shirts (the German-American Bund)—American reflections of European brands of Nazism and fascism—and individual mavericks, most prominently, Father Coughlin, who preached "social justice" and anticommunism from his center in Detroit. Grass-roots populism, also given new impetus by the Depression, focused on social justice, finding its spokesman in Huey P. Long, the Governor of Louisiana. Although both the Long movement and the more recent Wallace crusade were Southern expressions, appealing to the "forgotten man" and touching on related sentiments—anti big-business, anti big-government, anti big-city, and anti big-talk—they played different historical roles in their influence on and containment of radical protest in the United States. The populism of Governor Long was still linked to traditional Southern authoritarianism, which, however distorted and unrecognizable it had become, was in line with the tradition of the American rebellion. Viewing the movement within the context of the uneasiness of the thirties, it appeared to seek a return to American "decency" and to see its demands as part of the extension of the democratic ideal of equality. To this end, for example, Long's followers argued that the common man had to be protected against the abuses of rampant capitalist competition, and they led the fight for social-security legislation, old-age pensions and assistance, and health care. Their actions complemented (although they were in no way a part of) the demands being made on the national level by organized labor and its sympathizers. It was this type of parallel action on "felt" needs, however, which won F.D.R. his popular support and helped elect him to the presidency four times. Even though the populist appeal of Huey Long had antisocialist and antiunionist overtones, it was not specifically antiradical. Important to an understanding of its historical role is the fact that as a movement it remained contained within the South. It had little or no effect on the national protest scene, and except for its support of assistance programs, it had little effect on national social policy. The Wallace movement, on the other hand, although also rooted in rural, southern, and individualistic preindustrial traditions, blended this mixture with the discontents of the new, modern, industrialized South. Because it reflected the asymmetry of society as a whole, it found a response among those who felt "squeezed," giving the movement inordinant power to influence national policies, especially in the area of the containment of radical protest.

Possibly because of or despite these protest manifestations of both the Right and Left, but certainly because of massive discontent, the most important result of the thirties was the American public's disenchantment with *laissez-faire* capitalism and its political conservatism. In its stead it accepted a "managed" capitalism, couched in a viable and seemingly pervasive updated liberal politics. The Depression had destroyed the small entrepreneur— by 1940, only 18 percent of the population was self-employed—although the myth of being "in business for oneself" was not finally put to rest until after 1945. White-collar and professional government workers had, by the end of the war, become the symbol of the new Middle America, the "majority" group which had learned not only to accept but to expect social benefits from the national state.

Although New Deal subsidization had carried the country through the worst trough of the depression, World War II laid the foundation for recovery, affluence, and the full-fledged primacy of national politics. War economics has continued to delay a complete answer to the systemic questions posed in the thirties, and it may yet fall upon the seventies to complete or to review critically the domestic social engineering begun in the thirties. Nonetheless, the revival of the U.S. economy (pump-primed by the Marshall Plan and cold war) did serve to reawaken faith in the American creed of the pursuit of economic self-interest, a pursuit now tempered by the public's acceptance of state protection and regulation and by a realistic realignment between the sectors of production and distribution in their power (or interest) potential on the national, industrial marketplace. Fresh from the victory of overcoming the Nazi threat, the country, with renewed and unrelenting vigor, set out on the democratic mission to destroy the last remaining threat to the new capitalism—socialism. At home, this took on the face of McCarthyism and abroad the grimace of imperialism. Thus, the American traditions of democratic ethos and imperial colonialism were given new synthesis and new direction.

McCarthyism, much like the anti-Red campaign of the twenties, tapped and reshaped two typical American antiattitudes. First, antiestablishment and anti-intellectual populist sentiment was mobilized against the ideas of systemic flexibility and democratic participation of the Eastern intellectual "eggheads"; and second, antiradical and antiforeign sentiment was directed against all forms of socialism, communism, and political unionism. It also tapped the apolitical potential of extreme self-reliance which appeared to mask the lack of political identity and status anxiety of the new "hired hands"—the white-collar middle class. McCarthy's Permanent Subcommittee on Investigations of the Senate Committee on

Government Operations and its counterpart HUAC (Committee on Un-American Activities of the House of Representatives), although at first attacking only the small nucleus of the ideological Left, had, as was finally revealed, the broader target of vitiating the liberal politics initiated by Franklin Delano Roosevelt. Their covert goal seemed to be a revival of the idealized virtues of nineteenth-century America: individualism, religion, up-dated Puritan righteousness, and pragmatic know-how. In this sense, McCarthyism, as a political movement, must be seen as a conservative social critique of New Deal planning and the reequilibrated social order it had help create. Looked at from a long-range perspective, McCarthyism was the national expression of extreme Rightist protest sentiments. The depoliticization already begun as the last century ended, was furthered by the structural changes in class arrangements in the thirties, and, at least on the surface, was concretized during the McCarthy era by the added repression of political activism and radical criticism. The stage was set for another period of escapism. This time, however, unlike in the romantic twenties, escapism took the form of conscious withdrawal, and for some the final escape—suicide.

For those young people who came of age in the era of the antifascist war, liberalism had the added dimension of fervent antitotalitarianism. University-trained specialists, having been aroused by the war's mobilization themes of freedom and justice, followed Allen Dulles into the CIA and J. Edgar Hoover into the FBI to protect democracy from communism. It was in the era of McCarthyism that there developed a visible split between intellectuals who stayed outside the government, though for the most part working parallel to it, and those who wanted to be actively effective within it. The institutional stage of the latter group is defined by the fact that they sought and found a moral and political rationale for the decisions and actions (i.e., they are not yet part of a technocratic ideology). And it is this which separates them from "pure" technocrats who ignore this dimension, seeking absolution in ethical neutrality.

World War II also quickened and set the stage for important population shifts with far-reaching political consequences. After

1945, the South emerged as a revitalized urban and newly industrialized center ready to participate in shaping national politics.
Because of its new economic importance, the South could not be
kept encapsulated, nor would it allow itself to. With its admission
into the national polity as a full-fledged partner, Southern tradi-
tionalism and racist policies did much to aid and abet the McCarthy
thrust. The South's national constituency and influence was
complemented by—and perhaps found resonance because of—the
greatest overland migration in modern American history: the
movement of blacks to other parts of the country.* In answer to
war-production needs, thousands of blacks had been recruited to the
cities and industrial centers of the North and West, and they
brought with them rural habits and Southern tradition. By the late
fifties, as the migration turned into an exodus, their visibility
throughout the nation's major cities prompted responses which
made clear that racism was a national characteristic. The "Negro
problem" could no longer be confined to the ghetto of the South.
Since then, despite Supreme Court efforts to adjudicate the
problem, or the Executive's to ameliorate by decree or "benign
neglect," blacks have continued to confront the country with new
problems, controversies, and "hot issues" which seem to test and
prod the nation's democratic ethos.

According to the Bureau of the Census, the United States had
become a predominantly urban country by 1950. By the end of the
decade, the trickle of middle-class whites moving to the suburbs
begun in the thirties and forties, had become a flood spreading
urbanity and city problems throughout the country. Although this
second migration, which is still in progress, already far surpasses the
black transplantation, the two are complementary processes that
have created a "city" writ large. The suburb has become the habitat
of the "community of limited liability,"† hideaway and protective
coloration of the apolitical, while the nation's former cities have
become the locale of the "community of total liability."‡ Planners,
mayors, and urban riots have made it abundantly clear that not

---

* There have been three major black inland migrations: the first was in large measure due to
Reconstruction in the South; the second and third were due to the first and second world wars.
† See Scott Greer, *The Emerging City.*
‡ This phrase in an extension of Greer's concept.

only have the problems of the city merged with those of the nation, but that the long neglect of their physical and social plants and the disappearing middle-class tax base have also helped to turn urban centers into the social cancer of the nation. And the suburbs, much to the chagrin of the locals, show signs of not lagging too far behind.

The move to the green belt, however, does not mean that new suburbanites do not continue their ritualistic treks to the polls and their involvement in their local communities. They did and do. Their primary political concerns were the school, which they regulated and influenced through the PTA and other voluntary associations, and zoning, which they felt was necessary to protect their homes and property. As suburbanites grew in number and as new suburbs dotted the national map, their politics became national matters. Blacks also saw that their immediate political concern—winning a measure of control over their own lives—centered on the quality of education and available housing. It took less than twenty years for blacks and suburbanites to make their "gut issues" matters of national partisan politics and the rallying standards of dissent, radical protest, and backlash. Under the guise of decentralization, tax-sharing, and busing, the national-urban polity waged emotionally bitter battles that play a contrapuntal theme against the intense and sometimes violent protests waged by students on the nation's campuses.

Many suburbanites, at least in the early fifties, were not merely refugees from urban life but political exiles, and although they privately abhorred McCarthyism, they publicly accepted the limited-liability protection the suburb afforded them. These suburbanites, their liberalism learned in the thirties, coupled with the McCarthyite perspective learned in the fear-ridden atmosphere of the fifties and their forced retreat from national politics, found a substitute concern—the welfare of their immediate families. Out of this pragmatic and protective privatization was bred a new permissiveness for their young, which, so some have said, unwittingly laid the foundation for the resurgence of democratic radicalism in the sixties. By a sad twist of misunderstanding, Dr. Benjamin Spock, promoter of permissive child-rearing practices, has had to bear the brunt of the conservative displeasure with this young generation.

Having emerged from World War II as the most powerful noncommunist nation, the United States, in her foreign relations, turned to the task of protecting the democratic free world from the Soviet threat. Secure in the domestic economy's ability to ensure its continuing affluence by satisfying the public's stored-up desire for consumer products, President Truman and his successors brewed a second alphabet soup of containment—NATO (the North Atlantic Treaty Organization), SEATO (the South-East Asian Treaty Organization), and the OAS (Organization of American States). Encirclement and containment of world communism brought with it foreign economic aid, the necessary show of military force which involved the country in the Korean and Vietnam wars and the internal affairs of Guatemala, the Dominican Republic, Cuba, and Bolivia, and the increased counterinsurgency activities of the CIA. The domestic counterpart of these enterprises was the emphasis on greater vigilance and the broadened functions of the FBI and military-intelligence units. Although the excesses of McCarthy's crusade were disavowed in Washington, his concept of surveillance and governmental security continued to inspire and enlarge, however inconspicuously, the orbit of social activities subject to "internal protection."

In retrospect, the "cool and uncommitted" image of the fifties, a time of exhibitionistic anticommunism, appears to have been the shadow-boxing reflections of a deeper antagonism and a long-term historical trend—the apposition of the democratic ethos and imperial colonialism. One could perhaps better characterize the fifties as a period in which liberal leftists and conservative reactionaries seemed to retreat from direct confrontation, to silently gather new strength and find new strategies for another round of battle. It was in this ambience of relative political calm that a social-science school of thought embracing democratic plualism and the philosophy of the New Deal was elaborated. The traumatized young radicals of the thirties, now some twenty years older, having revisited and reexamined their disenchantment, presented their findings in conceptual form. One of their members, outlining the assumptions of the model, wrote: "democracy is not only or even primarily a means through which different groups can attain their

126

ends or seek the good society; it is the good society itself in operation."* Disappointed by the Stalinist distortions of Left ideology and impressed by the apparent absence of social tensions in the postwar welfare state, many of these former leftists proclaimed the irrelevancy of a radical Left in the sixties. For them the age of seeking a utopia had passed, and they viewed the day-to-day operations of democratic interchanges in the fifties as the flowering of the "new" nation's founding ideals.

The end-of-ideology doctrine of Daniel Bell and Seymour Lipset was not only, as we outlined earlier, a mere reflection of what we now recognize to have been a superficial reading of the existing mood of society, but also a doctrine based on a hopelessly blind disregard of the demographic changes taking place in the nation's cities; the persistence of racism, ghettoes, slums, poverty, and the emergence in the mid-fifties of a vocal and strong civil-rights movement. It is not surprising then that Harold Cruse, a black intellectual, could angrily comment on Bell's *End of Ideology*, "It seems almost incredible that in the face of a social movement of such dimensions that some people even call a revolution, a sociologist could write such a book and not even mention the existence of this movement or its impact."† Although the full resonance of the movement, admittedly, could not have been known at the time Bell was writing, he might have projected the politicization and radicalization of a vast number of black and white civil-rights workers as a possibility. Certainly, the very existence of this movement and, in light of the obviously untenable conditions of black life, its growing attraction for blacks, white liberals, and radicals, should have warned the prophets of the good society against proclaiming its advent. Now that we have witnessed the turmoil of the sixties, due in large measure to the blacks' determined insistence on betterment, the racial bias and the lack of analytical and conceptual objectivity of these social scientists becomes even more apparent.

With the end of the seemingly apolitical Eisenhower era, the fifties came to a fitful close. Not only was the black revolt growing,

* Seymour Martin Lipset, *Political Man*, p. 439.
† Harold Cruse, *The Crisis of the Negro Intellectual*, p. 460.

but other tension-producing problems were waiting in the wings. The political expression of these problems in the sixties was to lead to an ideological polarization of the American people. In the Presidential elections of 1960, a pump-primed society, affluent but punch-drunk from witch-hunts, geographical dislocations, and community disruptions, turned to a man promising a change in style and a reordering of priorities. John F. Kennedy, monied, zealous, personable, and knowledgeable about party and campaign politics (much in the FDR image) was chosen over Richard Nixon, Eisenhower's vice-president. In his inaugural address, Kennedy, feeling the pulse of the country's uneasiness, summoned the citizenry to purposeful action in the name of national community with the words, "Ask not what your country can do for you but rather what you can do for your country." Kennedy's platform and style, however, merely reflected and affirmed the changed nature of American society. Since the thirties, when New Deal social engineers had worked out nationwide solutions to deal with the problems of the Depression, the central government had assumed the function of organizing and ensuring rapid technological progress and economic growth. The new Chief Executive was now justifiably demanding the unquestioning loyalty of the citizens so that the state could move ahead with its assumed task. Apparently accepting the formula suggested by the end-of-ideology model, Kennedy further elaborated his technocratic approach to politics in 1962. Delivering a commencement address at Yale, he said: "The problems of the sixties as opposed to the kinds of problems we faced in the thirties demand subtle challenges for which technical answers—not political answers—must be provided." Kennedy, however, was to temper his lofty, cold, technocratic problem-solving strategies with emotional and humanistic tactics. In his short time in office, the words "commitment," "concern," and "human aid" became common political currency. They were to achieve even greater currency in the Great Society programs of President Johnson and were also to provide the New Left the weapons with which to probe, push, and shove the Liberal Establishment. We shall, of course, never know whether Kennedy's technocratic and humanistic goals would have been reconciled, but we do know that in the short run his humanism

128

failed. This was especially true as the narrow freedom spaces within which he worked became more apparent when his decisions to permit the Bay of Pigs adventure and increase the American presence in Indochina began to destroy the cohesiveness of the national polity which he had envisioned and so ardently demanded.

President Kennedy's acceptance of a viable relationship between the worlds of socialism and capitalism, carefully balanced by the continuation of Kennan's containment policy, was the foreign-relations component of his conciliatory yet technically oriented political style. His domestic relations were of the same fabric. At home he transferred the euphoric national sense of recommitment into the "new politics" of problem-solving. The New Frontier was to harness the never-ending fund of scientific and technological knowledge to the solutions of socioeconomic and political problems. Bright young men were called in from the universities and from the public-relations and research arms of industry to cut through time-consuming red tape in order to promote a rapid exchange of ideas and an immediate testing of policy suggestions. The expert hustle and bustle of New Frontiersmen, however, was to foreclose any chance of over-all assessment and critical evaluation of societal priorities for themselves as well as for the citizenry at large. Typical of the new technocratic style was the call on the social sciences for practical ways to mitigate the social impediments hampering New Frontier goals. Academics were given great importance, and, as they went in and out of government lending their approbation and expertise to social-policy decisions, intradisciplinary problems became more and more defined by political necessities. Spurred by an actively interested government and large federal grants, social scientists diligently went to work to answer the demands made on them. Not only did individual academics respond, but the university also felt called upon to review its institutional role vis-à-vis the state and society. Thus Clark Kerr, then president of the University of California, for example, pointed out that the multiversity was a service agency for government as well as other public interests. Some academic institutions, especially the more prestigious institutes of technology and larger state universities, were ready to answer government demands and quick to transfer their broad technical know-how to the social sciences. And they did so with amazing rapidity. The largest single scandal in the social sciences, a result of this scramble for large funds and willingness to serve political ends (and also perhaps because of the avaricious wish to preserve their newly gained status), was the counterinsurgency research of Project Camelot.* The exposure of the incident brought back shades of former uncertainties and much soul-searching to the social-science world.

In the past thirteen years, more and more social research and political attention has focused on the uses of education, the instrument which so often before in American history had served to bridge the gap between the contradictory strains of traditional goals and new needs. What has been called into question is whether the elastic faculty of education was perhaps becoming less flexible. Could it still remain the instrument to fulfill the democratic-ethos component of the American dream and, at the same time, be used to limit the uses of human freedom which this dream required? Could it serve both technocratic aims and humanistic needs? Although social scientists who were principally concerned with policy solutions of the New Frontier and the Great Society programs inadvertently, and for the most part unintentionally, posed the educational issue, the debate, picked up by intellectuals and academics, touched on tenets of the system itself. Effects of

---

* Project Camelot was the title of a contract research project of the Special Operations Research Office of the American University in Washington, D.C., supported by an initial $6 million grant from the Department of the Army. The research, which began in 1965, "projected an extremely broad look into at least half a dozen Latin American countries toward the end of isolating the conditions leading to internal revolt and deriving a set of conclusions indicating what could be done to contain or channel the effects of revolutionary disturbance. Historical as well as quantitative techniques were to be employed, and all sectors of society from schools to court systems and from paupers to presidents were to be analyzed." The Project's director sought and received advice from leading social scientists. The pilot run occurred in Chile, and it was there that Project Camelot was exposed. At first it caused mayhem only in academic circles, but with the American intervention in the Dominican Republic, its political overtones meshed with growing public opinion against interventionism and militarism and the "image of the United States as a power dedicated to the throttling of any revolutionary movement of whatever center-to-left stripe." Exposure of the project led to two Chilean investigative committees and investigation by the Congress of the United States, as well as resolutions by academic professional associations against the professoriate's involvement in government research. For a more complete analysis, see Kalman H. Silvert, "American Academic Ethics and Social Research Abroad," in his *The Conflict Society*, (New York: American Universities Field Staff, 1966).

130

social inequality were weighed against the costs of equality, which produced a debate about "integration," "culture of poverty," "cultural identity," "decentralization," and "benign neglect." At present, the controversy revolves around the political efficacy of meritocracy.

Between 1965 and 1967, young peoples' rejection of an impersonal technocratic society and their protest against the Vietnam war reached national proportions. So did race riots, the drug scene, white backlash, crime, pollution, and violence. As the American society was irrevocably made national, entire cities and university campuses became the new and uncontainable ghettoes, loci of total crisis. And the nation, caught in the vise of its contradictory traditions and modern times, grew restive and angry. The government's response, however, followed traditional administrative patterns: attempts to make these troubled and social problem areas invisible by encapsulation coupled with threats of containment by force. The treatment was a systematically applied mix of positive and negative sanctions—social-services and legal redress alternating with neglect and police action.

When Lyndon Johnson, schooled in the political corridors of the Senate and in the populism of the Democratic party, moved into the White House, he brought with him two Senatorial habits. In the Senate he had learned that regardless of differences between the Senators, matters of foreign-policy were predicated on a bipartisan commitment to the cold war; while domestic affairs, like local state politics, were predicated on the pragmatic desire to stay in office. Toward this end, one learned to keep a practiced eye on the electorate, and there is no reason to doubt that President Johnson, excellent practitioner of the Senatorial game that he was, was not aware of the political costs of a restless constituency. To reequilibrate the nation, he proposed the program of the Great Society. Based on the rather ingenious strategy of tapping the isolationist propensity of the American people in times of stress, he attempted tactically to separate foreign from domestic matters in the hope that moral sentiments could once again be focused solely on the obvious, but more compromisable, inequities at home—especially those which cut off access to the mainstream of middle-class life.

131

In the cities, however, the necessary instrumentalities of everyday life continued to play a clashing contrapuntal theme to established national priorities. Although space exploration and defense industry had produced a rapid acceleration of technological innovation, little if any of this new knowledge was applied to the fundamental spheres of health, education, housing, and transportation. Instead, as if to divert the public from these glaring inefficiencies but still open up avenues for their legitimate moral concerns, their attention was focused on ways to lend their individual assistance to the peoples of the Third World, to help in the fight against pollution, and to organize for consumer protection.

But neither the New Frontier nor the Great Society could stop disenchantment or protest, whether of the Right or the Left. The consensual basis of popular loyalty invoked by President Kennedy was rapidly turning into a myth: that is, for large groups of Americans, daily experience with the uneven development of vital sectors of society negated the existence of commonly shared national interests or politics. There seemed to be no question about the passing of the myth by the mid-sixties — the national society had lost its communal character. Group identity based on the ascribed characteristics of sex, race, and ethnicity was developing into new nuclei for the reestablishment of community and becoming the new instrumentality for social mobilization. Some social scientists saw in the demands for a return to the idea of "equality of result," a reincarnation of grass-roots populism. Here again, they argued, was a movement that questioned the presumption of individual talent and worth embodied in the concept of equality of opportunity. Others saw the rejection of strict individualism as a result of political and economic changes in the social system. Regardless of the impact of this new development on the idea of equality, war, which in the past had usually unified the nation and given it renewed communal purpose, in the late sixties fell on a differentiated populace quick to register the costs of war to their respective identity groups. To them the cost-benefit balance of the Vietnam war was obvious: the young, the blacks and the poor died or were maimed, while the public services vital to the well-being of their own communities were neglected or withheld. And while it is true that the development and wider use of mass-communication systems since 1945 had brought the nation closer together, in the sixties its facilities were used by these marginal groups to put the national polity on notice. By confrontation and argumentation, using reason and anger, they went on TV and radio and to the newspaper to spread the message that *their* politics was to create new standards for a new national consensus.

The blacks were the first challengers. During the fifties, under the leadership of the NAACP, they had painstakingly gone through the courts to seek legal help to make them part of the white consensus. But when legal decisions were blatantly contravened at all levels, their civil-rights struggle turned more virulent and they began to question the consensus itself. F.D.R.'s dictum, that there could be no government if one-third of the nation lived in economic deprivation appeared to apply equally to social deprivation. As it had been in the thirties, so it was in the sixties: there could be no national society without total mobilization and total inclusion—and because of racism, the nation was still in danger.

The second defection came from within the white community itself. More and more affluent, middle-class students began to see the consensus as a societal shield during the growth of a dehumanizing technocracy and they began to withhold their consent to be trained for the governing bureaucracies. Starting in small pockets of dissent even before the sixties—for the most part on the campuses of the Universities of California and Wisconsin—rebellious students drew attention to the fact that American society had undergone drastic structural changes whose impact on individual lives surfaced as these new characteristics became pervasive and overriding. The price was a "system"—now both bureaucratic and technocratic and abetted by the university establishment—which demanded an adaptive intelligence and stoic dedication to scientific problem-solving at the cost of public input and debate on social policies, a price they found reprehensible and self-defeating.

The political Right also joined in the attack. The new technocracy appeared to them to be contrived and spearheaded by an overpermissive establishment. They found its liberal patina, which they equated with the postindustrial elite, inimical to the fulfillment of America's destiny. As the decade progressed, the platform of the Right took shape. Generally they demanded an even stronger commitment to the American imperial mission abroad, a return to law and order at home, and an immediate halt to further racial integration. But neither the Republican party's swing to the extreme Right under Barry Goldwater in 1964 nor the growing Wallace movement could muster enough strength to recreate the comforting consensus of former times or stem the tide of rebellion. Their reactions merely helped to exacerbate political polarization and speed up the erosion of the national community.

In the winter of 1968–69, with the accumulation and quick succession of what had at first seemed isolated and local occurrences in Berkeley (1964), Watts (1964 and 1965), and Detroit (1967), and with the founding of a militant Black Power movement (1967), massive peace demonstrations in the national capital and other major cities (1968–69), the murder of Martin Luther King, Jr., and the subsequent riots, and escalating campus unrest across the nation, it became impossible for the government or the public to ignore the instability of the union any longer. By the end of the decade, many Americans felt that the entire nation had assumed the basic characteristics of a slum; not only was there a national crisis, but more important, everybody knew it!

1967 saw social scientists—adherents of the model of democratic pluralism who at the turn of the decade had seen little or no indications of student or societal unrest in the foreseeable future—ready to give their account of the unexpected return of radical dissent. Their analyses were generally of a piece: the societal disequilibrium was related to basic systemic changes, causing the emergence of a new society which they variously labeled "postindustrial," "technological," "cybernetic," or "technetronic"; thus, dislocations and protests were but symptoms of rapid change, rebellious in character, perhaps, but not potentially revolutionary. Satisfied with their reassessment of the situation and *their* moral sentiments, the advocates of the end-of-ideology thesis concluded that the addition of new technological components did not change the underlying theme of their fifties proposition: democratic pluralism was still the model of the future society.

The postindustrial explanation shared a premise with the arguments presented by early student leaders and their prophet, philosopher Herbert Marcuse, whose strategy of the "Great Refusal"* fitted their first blush of frustration in 1964. They, too, separated technical innovation from its economic base and invested it with an animus of its own. But by 1967, disaffected students, blacks, and others who had joined their ranks, had already begun to reevaluate their original analyses and redirect their passions. In this painful history of reassessment and protest action and in the reactions of their mentors lie many of the roots of the ideological differences between today's intellectual and political protagonists in the debate on inequality and the future of democratic life. In the social sciences, the climate of the past fifteen years has led to a weakening of the neopositivistic stranglehold and to the growing importance of the alternative ideas embodied in phenomenology, ethnomethodology, and Marxism.

Daniel Bell has rightly emphasized the importance of new technological advances on the future relationship between work and leisure. His analysis does not break the chain of the classical economic tradition which holds that conditions of "work" are the result of production, regulated by a supply-and-demand market-place and fueled by the competitive spirit to maximize monetary (and power) returns. He has, however, disengaged economic motives from moral sentiments—the positive linkage upon which Adam Smith was to elaborate the "naturalness" and "goodness" of *his* concept of capitalist enterprise*—by replacing Smith's regulating sentiments with a non-human determinant which he calls the "centrality of knowledge." With this judicious substitution, Bell has not only finally found a way to free the classical formulation from its ties to "higher" human motives, but has also rid us of the source of ideological, chiliastic passions, a task he apparently had not quite completed when he wrote *The End of Ideology* in 1960.

* Marcuse suggested in *One-Dimensional Man* that the enlightened person's only response to the oppressive force of technological rationality was to withdraw from or actively hinder the successful imposition of such a system. He called it the Great Refusal. For a more specific discussion of the bases of his reasoning, see p. 00.

* The fact that Smith's reliance on morality is also questionable is irrelevant to the point being made here.

Following this release from the confining limits of the old political-economy model, Daniel Bell and others of his persuasion have advanced the argument that universities are well on the way towards becoming the paramount institutions of modern society, because they generate the theoretical and technical knowledge so important for the maintenance of continued economic growth. Thus, in the postindustrial world, the university has a clear and pure productive function, and social change—now only a matter of complex though attainable know-how—is created by the technical elites residing within its walls. (Residence, however, is not a continuing requirement. What is important is that these elites be trained and socialized in the institution.) Politics obviously becomes more and more subject to scientific expertise and is intruded upon by technocratic decisions, guided only by scientific and technical laws and oriented toward the planning and management of the future. Nonetheless, these social scientists continue to project a belief in democratic pluralism and see a certain amount of public participation in the choice of this or that solution. Although their rehabilitated model accounts for the new innovative factor and identifies the newer agencies of social-technical change, capitalism as a source of power and a limitation of social organizational modes is ignored rather than confronted, but then, so had it also been in its generic formulation. Under the guise of a purely political theory (the economic sector having been neutralized*), politics as a process of mediation of group pressures is turned into an arena of pure decision-making. But old-fashioned politics are not to be forgotten or shelved. Politicians are still needed to mediate ways and means for bringing previously excluded marginal groups into the national polity. For all other "problems," however, they see traditional liberal politics transformed into the consensual bond of a new technocratic culture; while progress, another traditional passion not to be discarded out of hand, now underwritten as "a faith in security through technological knowledge," remains the magic password to the future. The question of the search for a better-structured human order (what the utopian classicists called a more godlike order, or later centuries, a more humane order) and the existential question of

* Ralf Dahrendorf was perhaps the first to lay the groundwork of this neutralization thesis in the early fifties.

136

"becoming" (the wider discovery of human potential), which together have sparked critical attacks on all suggested rationalizations of the "universality" and "rightness" of existing social inequities, have once again been put to rest by making "merit" (the once-removed objective measure of human potential) accountable only to the needs and preferred knowledge of technical know-how.

The implication that the individual pursuit-of-merit rewards, regulated by technical necessities, will, in the long run, better satisfy material human wants and the community at large leans heavily on a devitalized restatement of Adam Smith's moral precepts and only begs the question. Bell's proposition that postindustrial man's quest for utopia resides not in human consciousness or collective formulations derived from historical experience but solely on the "stage" of technical progress brings us back to the divergent paths (and goals) chosen by these social scientists and student protesters. The students' fight was waged specifically *against* this denial of utopia. Said Mario Savio in 1964:

> The university is the place where people begin to question the condition of their existence and raise the issue whether they can be committed to the society they have been born into. After a long period of apathy ... students began not only to question, but having arrived at answers, to act on their answers. This is part of a growing understanding among people in America that history has not ended, that a better society is possible, and that it is worth dying for.*

Social scientists who agreed with Savio that the end-of-ideology argument was mistaken and who also found the reworked democratic pluralism model which flowed from it wanting, have alternative explanations for the crisis which confronts the American people. They agree with their colleagues that technical changes have occurred and that qualitative leaps are necessary. But in their view, the agency for a transformation is to be found in the class structure which has as yet not been altered (and they believe never will be) by a "superimposed" technology. Generally, those who think along these lines are Neomarxists, but even among them there are

* *Humanity*, Dec. 1964, edited version of a tape recording made by Mr. Savio during the Sproul Hall sit-in at Berkeley University in California.

important differences, as we have noted in another section. Some see the potential in the alienation of the growing number of peripheral groups—marginal persons expendable and unnecessary to the "central productive process of the U.S. economy"*—while others contend that the potential is to be found in the newly politicized intellectuals and students.†

While social scientists in their analyses responded to American society's crisis in terms of their individual liberal or radical perspectives, politicians were caught between Left confrontation and Right backlash. They were faced with the immediate necessity of coping with a growing polarization which threatened to turn the streets of the nation into places of open warfare. For many persons in different walks of life, this polarization, fed by the escalating violence of the Vietnamese war (as well as their government's disregard of the majority's desire to quit the war) and the violence of inequities in urban life both to blacks and whites (as well as their government's seeming inability or unwillingness to grapple with its causes) was to destroy the end-of-ideology myth once and for all. For the first time in American history, Marxist social criticism became more widespread among the general public. Black militants, women, students, intellectuals, social scientists, and grass-roots populists were infused with the "new radicalism."‡ Ideological differences between the Republican and Democratic parties, which since World War II had become merely a slight set of differences between status groups, were, so to speak, reborn. As the sixties grew older it became more and more evident that their developing differences centered on the emphasis each gave to one or the other national traditions: imperial colonialism was becoming the core of Republican reaction, while the democratic ethos was to be central to dissident Democrats who rallied to the standards of Eugene McCarthy and George McGovern. Each party was to tug at the federal, frustrated frantic citizen—the squeezed and allegedly silent, choiceless white and blue-collar worker.

* See Jean Baker Miller, "On Women: New Political Directions for Women," Social Policy, II, No. 2 (July-August, 1971).

† See Herbert Marcuse, Counterrevolution and Revolt (Boston: Beacon Press, 1970).

‡ The Partisan Review unfortunately did not have a real scoop in its 1964 edition. It called the new trend the "New radicalism"; instead, it became known as the New Left.

The Republican party was the first of the two to try its hand at ideological politics. In the presidential campaign of 1964, Senator Barry Goldwater of Arizona ran as the party's standard bearer in the far Right's bid to capture both the party and the nation. Although he was overwhelmingly rejected by the American voter, his campaign gave form and organization as well as party recognition to the ideology which it later hammered into a successful platform. The aborted move also helped make Governor George Wallace a power to be reckoned within the Democratic party, which in turn helped the Republican's recruitment drive in the formerly solidly Democratic South. Obviously important to the realignment of ideological centers between the two major parties was the new-found political strength of the South. The Republicans took the initiative, resourcefully tapping the region's conservative and populist bent by dovetailing their "Southern strategy" with an appeal to the "silent majority," those dissenters who, according to Republican reckoning, had for so long been unable to voice their protest and whom the party now hoped to mold into its new constituency. The strategy worked. The stage was set for Richard Nixon's return to national politics,* and he captured the Presidency in 1968 running as a right-centrist champion of grass-roots Amer-ican conservatism. With his victory, it became evident that the democratic ethos was to become subject to the necessary constraints of the greater national mission of manifest destiny.

Meanwhile, the Democratic party floundered, unable to fulfill the promises of the Great Society or to bring the Vietnam war to an end. President Johnson, bowing to radical disavowal and public frustra-tion, declared he would not seek another term. Although old-line party leaders controlled Congress, they were unable to keep the traditional Democratic constituency intact. After an eight-year tenure, as it began to prepare for the 1968 national elections, the Democratic party found itself in the anomolous position of being the underdog. The party, having largely lost its traditional base as the party of the working man, the newly arrived immigrant, and the South, consciously began to redefine its position only after Eugene

---

* Richard Nixon had been defeated by John Kennedy in 1960 and by the democratic machine in the California gubernatorial race in 1962.

McCarthy marched through the Democratic primaries, proving that disaffected young people could still be rallied to the party if it showed committed concern. Yet important sectors of the party did not face up to the necessity of seeking a new basis of coalition until after the Chicago disturbances at their convention later that summer and the tremendous credibility gap of the Humphrey campaign. By the time the party gathered for its 1972 convention in Florida, dissident Democratic leaders had assumed control and brought with them a new formula for coalition—*quota democracy*. Defined in broad terms, theirs was a two-part proposition: the representation of all minority and marginal groups in proportion to the general population and the representation of their interests in proportion to their power to persuade each other that their grievances fit the general persuasion of all. Following the Democratic party's traditional role of champion of the underdog, dissident Democrats once again tried to respond to the expressed political needs of marginal groups by heeding their radical populist call to the democratic ethos. As the new antiwar party, it chose George McGovern (who like Eugene McCarthy had sought grass-roots support by campaigning in the state primaries) to head its slate—a man whose declared first priority was to end the American involvement in Vietnam. The Democratic Young Turks' choice of tapping an ingenious American accommodation (the permissive cultural and group identification of its heterogeneous ethnic and multiracial population), and of trying to turn the accommodation's potentially exclusive character into a basis for coalition was, perhaps, an intuitive attempt to grapple with an unresolved American dilemma. On the other hand, it was yet another example of the ability of the American polity to keep the full strength of group consciousness bottled up. Although it may not have been by grand design, the Democratic party's return to ideological politics—mixing a recognition of the colonial nature of the undeclared war in Southeast Asia and the widened distance between the classes and races at home—was the first attempt by a major American party to resolve the contradictory legacy of its twin traditions with the view of fulfilling the democratic promises of their rebellious forefathers.

Selected Bibliography

Chapter Nine

Bailyn, Bernard, *The Origins of American Politics*. New York: Vintage Books, 1968.

Baran, Paul A., and Paul M. Sweezy, *Monopoly Capital*. New York: Monthly Review Press, Modern Reader Paperback Edition, 1968.

Bell, Daniel. *The End of Ideology*. New York: The Free Press, 1960.

Bernstein, Barton J. (ed.). *Towards a New Past: Dissenting Essays in American History*. New York: Random House, Vintage Books Edition, 1969.

Cruse, Harold. *The Crisis of the Negro Intellectual*. New York: William Morrow, Apollo Editions, 1967.

Forman, Robert E. *Black Ghettos, White Ghettos, and Slums*. Englewood Cliffs, N.J.: Prentice-Hall, 1971.

Halberstam, David. *The Best and the Brightest*. New York: Random House, 1971.

Lipset, Seymour Martin. *Political Man*. Garden City, N.Y.: Doubleday & Co., 1960.

___. *The First New Nation*. Garden City, N.Y.: Doubleday & Co., 1963.

Lynd, Staughton. *Intellectual Origins of American Radicalism*. New York: Random House, Vintage Books Edition, 1969.

Mills, C. Wright. *White Collar: The American Middle Classes*. New York: Oxford University Press, 1951.

___. *The Power Elite*. New York: Oxford University Press, 1956.

Nieburg, H. L. *In the Name of Science* (rev. ed.). Chicago: Quadrangle Paperbooks, 1970.

Rischin, Moses (ed.). *The American Gospel of Success*. Chicago: Quadrangle Paperbooks, 1965.

Schirmer, Daniel R. *Republic or Empire*. Cambridge, Mass.: Schenkman Publishing Co., 1972.

Schonfield, Andrew. *Modern Capitalism*. New York: Oxford University Press, 1965.

Symes, Lillian and Travers Clement. *Rebel America*. Boston: Beacon Press, 1972.

Tindall, George B. *The Emergence of the New South: 1913-1945*. Baton Rouge: Louisiana State University Press, 1967.

Williams, William Appleman. *The Roots of the Modern American Empire*. New York: Random House, 1969.

___. *The Tragedy of American Diplomacy*. New York: Delta Book, 1972.

III

MAINSTREAM
AND REVOLUTION

10
PERSPECTIVES ON RADICAL CHANGE IN AMERICA

I

    Social scientists of different theoretical and political persuasions are agreed that modern capitalist states concentrate their greatest efforts on the tension-management of three continually challenging conflict areas. The first of these is the complex of economic stability or economic crises; the second, the economic, political, and military aspects of foreign relations (i.e., imperialism, war, etc.,); and the third, class struggle or group conflict.[1] In the past, crises in these sensitive areas generally occurred successively and so could be resolved serially. However, these resolutions were illusory, for no sooner was one problem mastered when another cropped up. In the sixties, the glaring results of asymmetrical development did away with the relative luxury of piecemeal solutions. For the first time in its history, the United States became the scene of a cumulative as well as simultaneous crisis situation in all three areas, one that demanded either a multifaceted program of crisis management, to which the system responded first with the Great Society concept, and then with the autocratic, corporate reorganization of authority and the state under the guise of the New Federalism, or a strategy for radical social change from those protest-prone groups that were or could be mobilized.

In our review of the historical development of the American system we focused on the interplay of integrating efforts and radical dissent, because, in our view, conflict and change are dialectically connected with stabilization and integration. To pursue the second alternative—the question of the prospects of revolutionary change—requires an assessment of the consciousness and power base of protest groups and the same dialectic connection.

II

During the past decade, interest in social change and protest against untenable conditions have primarily been articulated and acted out by groups organized around the ascribed characteristics of race, ethnicity, sex, and age. These ascribed status groups emphasize "identity" as one of their major group goals, which, expressed in cultural terms, serves as a platform for group-oriented and group-centered "political" action to attain access to the system. Even the so-called counterculture, because of its special association with youth, can be seen as a variety of the cultural group consciousness.

The current emphasis on cultural identity parallels that facet of the American tradition based on a grass-roots folklore, the sentiment of antiurban naturalism and the history of ethnic and "subcultural" politics. Most of the groups seeking a cultural identity and proclaiming their own cultural heritage have been marginal to or excluded from the so-called high culture (except for the troublesome instance of white middle-class students). Thus, in the cultural realm, we have seen a turnabout. Deprivation by exclusion or marginality status has brought to the surface what has always been a latent part of the American myth: the inherent goodness and justified existence of the "culture" of all groups and people.

The emergence of ascribed group-consciousness, however, at present seems to provide merely a potential base for collective solidarity and action in the political realm, one whose possible threat to the existing arrangements is still uncertain. Current

146

evidence suggests, for instance, that the new group-consciousness may merely be a shell within which individualism in the traditional form is sustained. Perhaps the most telling example of this possibility is that those who tend to be most interested in "doing their own thing" are the very persons who proclaim group membership.

It must of course be remembered that individualism in the American sense has two facets: *egotism* as the pursuit of largely economic self-interest leading to competition in the market-place, and *individuality* as the "stubborn" adherence to certain basic democratic rights (especially those referring to the individual person and to the community) leading to often unexpected rebellious acts of individuals, who have to be reckoned with as "idiosyncratic personalities" (cf. New England rebels). In terms of a strategy of radical change, political organizers will somehow have to overcome the "egotism" aspect of American individualism. But they would be hard put and possibly self-defeating if they tried to eliminate the second aspect altogether. If individualism in its idiosyncratic tradition can be tapped and incorporated into group-consciousness, it would serve as the hitherto missing safeguard against the development or imposition of authoritation structures, which has been a divisive (and a destructive) force among the Left. But the idiosyncratic tradition presents a problem in itself. If it is brought into play against the development of organized group activities *per se* (i.e., only because of the organization involved), it would destroy the development of collective political work at the very outset. This relationship between individuality and organized group activity has been a critical factor for many antiauthoritarian youth groups whose ineffectual organization has been criticized by more "disciplined" (and authoritarian) political activists. To create a viable synthesis of individuality and organization seems to be one of the major tasks facing American dissenters. Giving up the first would mean giving up a valuable part of the American tradition.* But without the latter, protest would be doomed.

* Women's groups are a case in point. Their emphasis on personal and "cultural" identity has led to forms of activities and expressions which possibly might destroy individuality in the above sense. At present, most consciousness-raising sessions and T-groups seem to deny the very conditions essential to the development and maintenance of individuality: privacy and the recognized right to idiosyncratic behavior.

As long as protest groups remain concerned with defining themselves on the basis of ascribed characteristics, we would suggest that they are in a *prepoliticization* stage. This does not, however, deny the political importance of the issues they raise: the quest and demand for possibilities to voice genuine needs repressed by a commercialized culture, and building a new and undistorted identity. Further development hinges, it seems, on whether they will recognize their *common* condition vis-à-vis the established societal order. This means that intragroup concerns and identity problems would have to lose their prominence and become relative though possibly necessary stages in the development of full politicization. Getting over the hurdle of prepoliticization apparently demands an analysis of the protest groups' specific socioeconomic, political, and cultural condition, a review of their demands and goals as well as their power base and strategies in relation to the total society. Then identity as a goal of free self-realization—liberation of needs—might turn into a political issue as well.

The current objective constellation in the United States, it seems to us, contains the possibility, however faint, that some of the protest-prone groups (or perhaps only some of their members) will be provoked to undergo a political learning process which would enable them to link their directly experienced needs and interests and the abstract* condition of societal totality and structure. This in turn, would then help to redefine their needs and interests. Once having chosen this path, they might realize that lower pay, underemployment, and unemployment for white middle-class women and the ghetto population are merely expressions of a very similar exploitation. Even at this point, it has become increasingly evident that on the basis of its minimal economic power, neither group can gain economic or political advantage nor realize its interests, whatever these may be and however they may vary. This learning process might also lead to the realization that exploitation and oppression are neither limited to marginal groups nor to their most apparent, elementary, and brutal forms, which are readily identifiable, agreed upon, and often mentioned. Many persons, for instance, in the ascribed category "white males"—and as such often

---

* "Abstract" in the sense that the total society cannot be directly "experienced" by an individual.

attacked by blacks and other marginal groups—may also be seen as being subject to exploitation, alienation, and oppression in the form of authoritarian work situation, unrelenting competition, and pressure to perform and achieve. The responses to and the effects of these conditions may be primarily psychological (stress, anxiety, and neurosis, for example) and thus more subtle, but certainly no less real than poverty or status deprivation. In other words, to bring about a change in these marginal groups from a prepoliticization stage to full political consciousness, the learning process would have to comprehend the phenomena of racism and sexism within the framework of a class analysis of American society. Short of this group consciousness remains more of a divisive factor, and given the traditional play of pluralistic interest groups, tends to immunize or neutralize its potential as a source of macrosocial change.

On the other hand, groups that have developed some measure of revolutionary *political* consciousness and reached out to make common cause with others have been threatened in their very existence not only by the establishment, but also by rival "brother" groups (i.e., groups organized around the same ascribed characteristics), still primarily concerned with their separate identities and exclusively committed to fighting what they perceive as their specific cause.

The Black Panther Party is a case in point. The black movement of the fifties and sixties has, as we know, produced not only different formulations of group goals but also competing groups. The civil rights movement headed by Martin Luther King, Jr., pursued an integrationist goal, focusing on broadened access of blacks to white institutions. King believed that the American system would respond favorably to his moral exhortations and nonviolent, integrated marches. His position, however, was challenged by the separatism advocated by the Black Muslims, which articulated in cultural and religious terms, found its corollary in an international perspective: the cultural identity of the Black African, Islamic, and American black nations. The ultimate demand of the Black Muslims, although not practically pursued, is geographic separatism. The resurgence of such black separatist movements throughout American history can ultimately be traced to the separate interests of the

Negroes, who were forcibly brought to this country during the colonial period.

Black Power, as proclaimed by Carmichael and Hamilton,[2] secularized many of the themes espoused by the Nation of Islam and combined the search for a cultural and religious black identity with the demand for the political and economic self-determination of black people in their own communities. With this, the emphasis shifted from the demand for a separate black nation in the South to the call for the creation of autonomous black enclaves in which blacks could build their own economic, political, social, and cultural institutions. But Carmichael and Hamilton spoke "of blacks receiving a proportionate share of societal power ... not of a total change in power distribution .... [And] their failure to clearly specify the values and goals in terms of which the ghetto is to be transformed has allowed a number of alternate definitions of black power to develop. Among them is the very nonrevolutionary concept of black capitalism or the creation of a parallel capitalism in the ghetto."[3] In their everyday operations, Black Power activists have advocated community control of educational and welfare institutions. Their emphasis is on their own communitites: a nationwide revolution is not immediate to them because, by and large, the white majority of America in their view is not subject to the exploitation and dehumanizing effects of the system.

The belief that blacks can resolve their own situation without a total redistribution of power on the national scale and without the destruction of capitalism has been challenged by the Black Panther Party, for whom the liberation struggle will and must take place in the form of a socialist revolution against capitalism, imperialism, and colonialism, and not as a struggle between blacks and whites. "The Black Panther Party knows that racism has always existed in lower forms, but that capitalism has institutionalized, commercialized, and mass-produced racism to such a high degree that it is sometimes thought of as a separate entity."[4] And "not only are blacks kept in a slave condition, all persons in this country are essentially in that condition."[5] With these theoretical insights and the slogan "All Power to the People" calling for the liberation of all citizens, the Black Panther Party presented a serious ideological challenge to the established power arrangements. At the same time, however, it also made itself suspect to cultural and political black nationalists who rejected any cooperation with whites. Although small in number, the Black Panther movement was perceived as an imminent threat to the system and has been subjected to systematic persecution.*

Puerto Rican, Chicano, American Indian, and feminist groups have a similar history of coexisting liberal-integrationist, cultural-separatist, and political-revolutionary positions. Among them, the most widespread support is given to what might best be called a cultural trade-unionism of the deprived. In the colleges, for example, various groups compete for their respective studies programs and for scholarship funds or positions for their members. At times, various marginal groups form coalitions based on commonly shared inequities and grievances. For the most part, however, the demands of these separate groups or coalitions leave the institutional arrangements untouched: access to labor and consumer markets and the development of a viable collective and individual identity are the primary goals. Accepting the argument of the allegedly existing scarcity of funds or job openings, they fall back on their group-centered self-interests, since their demands are still of a conservative bent,† making coalitions of marginal groups prone to disintegration. Despite this, the very possibility of a coalition of *all* marginal groups is increasingly invoked as a symbolic threat to the system—a threat to overwhelm the powers that be by sheer and ever-increasing numbers of expendable people. While the search for a new, undistorted identity and the pursuit of economic and political self-interests remain dominant in the various groups, they often, for tactical purposes, it would seem, speak of the desirability of a broad coalition. Put another way, they call for cooperation not so much out of concern for other equally oppressed, excluded, and discriminated-against groups, but rather in recognition that such a coalition would strengthen their power base and increase their conflict potential.

* This has not only resulted in a split of the party, but more recently also in a seeming cooptation of one of its founders: in 1973, Bobby Seale ran for the office of mayor in Oakland, California.
† Conservative in the sense that they do not challenge the essential nature of the institutional or socioeconomic structures.

151

Even if a large number of marginal people were mobilized and had a revolutionary consciousness, one would have to concede that their major threat would consist only of *ideological delegitimations*. That is (and always with the proviso that these persons could resist the countervailing forces of persuasion and cooptation), the American myth, the notion of national community, and the liberal image of a pluralist democracy would eventually lose credibility and plausibility. But mobilization and delegitimization would not complete the process. If, however, the American myths were in fact actually to lose legitimacy, then the power of debunking ideologies could, in the long run, turn into real political power. There is another proviso to this second phase, namely, that the countervailing response would not have led to the successful constraint of a full-blown totalitarian state.

The potential power base of marginal groups is most weakened by their relative or absolute lack of functional importance to the perpetuation of the system. They cannot threaten to refuse to cooperate because they do not cooperate in the first place, or, at best, only marginally. They do, however, take on importance in their function as consumers, which might provide the structural base for their heightened radical consciousness. But even this function can be regulated by political authorities through welfare restrictions and ameliorating social policies (e.g. work-requirement stipulations for welfare payments, minimum guaranteed income, etc.). Thus marginal groups, especially the impoverished, have little chance to use the consumer weapon without becoming self-defeating, and a sustained boycott of consumer goods by marginal groups with greater income flexibility is also highly improbable.

Regulating the poor is particularly required in times of economic decline, when structural unemployment cannot be counteracted by the reduction of work time. In this situation, the state must prevent or weaken the internalization of the work ethic among a significant number of persons. Such a devaluation of capitalist values, however, must be limited to specific and clearly identifiable groups which can be depicted as being psychosocially and culturally distinct. In this way, the myth of the validity of capitalist culture can be sustained and further strengthened by the efforts of social workers to develop

152

the capacity for self-improvement among the poor and excluded (in much the same way as psychoanalysis has been applied to the middle class). The "social marginality"[6] discussed by some Latin American social scientists in their early explorations—marginality resulting from allegedly distinct characteristics of groups, thus leading to a dualism (parallel separateness) between marginals and nonmarginals—can be viewed as a necessary and available political-ideological tool in the struggle for stabilizing the U.S. economy.

A policy based on the false notion of a naturally existing social marginality is effective as long as racism—and black separatism—support it ideologically by invoking the psychosocial and cultural distinctness of blacks. It becomes even more successful when social marginality is generated through economic deprivation or drugs. The resultant apathy and social disorganization gives rise to the other part of the social-marginality equation described in the literature.

Women are the targets of a similar strategy, which among the middle class results in a curious contradiction: while they are expected to transmit the values of capitalism to their children, they are discouraged or prevented from translating their own belief in these values—a prerequisite for adequate child-rearing—into an active participation in the labor market. Again, the idea of their "distinct" characteristics is invoked.

Speaking more directly of sources of power other than delegitimations and consumer function, we would like to discuss the idea of power base in its connotation of usurpation of space or "turf," as advanced by separatism. The concentration of blacks and other racial groups in the inner cities, the increased control of educational and welfare institutions by minority groups in urban centers, and the vulnerability of the larger cities to violence or guerrilla warfare are often cited in this regard. But the exodus of big corporations to the suburbs and the trend toward organizational decentralization of mega-administrations and bureaucracies has called into question the strategic importance of the inner city.* The concept of power

* In this connection mention should be made of central business district (CBD) reinvestment to save "old wealth" and to the current trend toward capital disinvestment in recognition of

derived from territorial occupation becomes even more difficult to implement, it seems to us, with the increasing importance of multinational corporations that transcend the narrow boundaries of nation-states, let alone cities, and make it ever more difficult for urban guerrilla groups to identify suitable targets of attack. In light of this shift in economic power, if a radical consciousness and cohesive political organization are to develop among marginal groups, then these must take quantum leaps to match this rearrangement. The imperative leap applies equally to the nations of the Third World. Within the politics of socialism, this trend brings to the fore an unresolved problem which has plagued the Left for a long time: the possible emergence of an *international* revolutionary consciousnes . Although it would appear that multinational corporations (and metropolitan nodes) would make this type of consciousness more imminent, it becomes equally apparent that this would require blacks and other marginal groups in the United States, for example, to skip a phase of economic-political development and experience which the majority of the people have lived through—that is, to by-pass the experience of an economically comfortable middle-class existence within the capitalist system. Implicit in such a demand is the notion that twentieth-century responses to exploitation, alienation, and marginality must be intrinsically different from those known in the nineteenth-century, as well as the rejection of a simplistic determinism. And it calls for persons who, because of their intellectual potential, can emancipate themselves from their immediate conditions, even if these tend to hold individuals in a double-bind situation.* In the case of blacks and other marginal ethnic and racial groups, the odds against such an emancipation are great but not insurmountable, as has been demonstrated by parts of the black movement in the sixties. The longer these groups continue, however, to think along lines of access and ethnic politics as opposed to class politics, the less important

the concept of "insured risk" in the shift of economic power now based on the dispersed geographical complex of corporate holdings.

* The concept of the double-bind situation has been developed by scientists doing research on schizophrenia (Bateson *et alii*). In terms of structural situations, it denotes the contradictory nature and mutual exclusiveness of simultaneous behavior patterns demanded by a given situation; specific sanctions if the demands are not met; and the impossibility to escape this condition.[7]

will be their role in the eventual transformation of this society. Various reasons for this exist:

1. The loss of strategic advantages due to the changing nature of the inner cities[8] and development of multinational corporations.

2. The likely cooptation of their educated leaders.

3. The time and opportunity for the state to organize more effectively and make provision for the suppression of eventual revolts and the containment of the ghettoes.*

4. The impossibility of affecting a redistribution of power on the national level without winning the support of all ethnic as well as nonmarginal groups.

5. A regressive political learning process resulting from the continual disappointment of individual and collective hopes, fear, and the effects of permanent poverty and cultural deprivation.

On the other hand, one should not discount the radical potential of access politics. Although the reformist approach usually leads to partial success and only temporary integration, such partially successful political experiences may easily stimulate new learning processes, leading in turn to new conflicts fed by still unsatisfied needs. But the "success" of ascribed access politics to satisfy consumer needs that disregard the identity problem (ego needs) and ignore the need for self-expression and self-determination is likely to bring mere temporary pacification. The various turns in the development of the black movement is a striking example of the dialectics inherent in the politics of partial successes. The American system which operates on the principle of economic rewards as the means for such partial conflict resolutions will find it increasingly more difficult to legitimate systemic compromises to satisfy non-economic needs.

The large reformist civil-rights groups have also been important to protest formation in terms of a ready organization which has often provided the structural nucleus around which more loosely organized mass movements and transitory demonstrations could develop.† Confirmed individualists such as intellectuals, as well as

---

* Expanded police forces and increased state expenditures for arming and training them are indications of an accelerating class struggle from above.

† Cf. the role of the black civil-rights movement in the development of student protest and spontaneous mass demonstrations.

the constantly fluctuating mass of students, for example, can temporarily "lean" on such organizations and utilize them for their own political struggle, and thus no longer fight in isolation. But in order to stabilize their success, these intellectuals and students have to remain organized. Political organizations, not spontaneous street demonstrations, would provide the construct for the development of a political tradition and the integration of their collective experiences—result of their learning processes as well as their critical discussion—and favor the development of a historical-political consciousness of individual members. This, in turn might stimulate new political praxis. For this to happen, however, political organizations must take care not to be rigid, authoritarian, or dogmatic, or superimpose their goals on nonpolitical or "prepolitical" individuals whose needs most often surface in disorganized demonstrations.

Organized access politics, if viewed from this dialectical perspective, may in the long run be the basis of a revolutionary potential. But for the present, and in the short haul, this strategy lends greater credence to the continued viability of a democratic pluralism and to the belief of an open society in which individuals as group members can still "make it" if only given the opportunity.

III

Blacks and other nonwhites have voiced their desires for equal opportunities for a long time, especially after the black exodus from the South, the greater influx of Puerto Ricans to the East coast and the larger concentration of Mexicans in the Southwest. In the pursuit of access politics, these groups have often echoed the old American faith that "education could be used as a tool to reduce inequality in society."[9] In the sixties, liberal Democrats vigorously pushed for specific social policies and administrative measures designed to answer these demands.[10] Although many protest-prone marginal groups still continue to focus on education as a means for upward mobility, the underlying ideology and so-called success of liberal educational policies have become the subject of social-scientific controversy and heated political debates. Many of the supposedly realistic reassessments of the relationship between mobility and educational opportunity furnished the Nixon Administration with justifications for cutting public expenditures for education.[11]

The controversy started in 1966, when the results of a massive empirical survey of schools, students, and teachers (the Coleman report)[12] seemed to fly in the face of the common wisdom. The report's major finding suggested that differences in family background rather than schools* accounted for the differential achievements of the various racial and ethnic groups. In the dispute about the possible policy effects of the findings, quantitative empirical research—which scientifically minded sociologists of the positivist persuasion consider the most objective basis for scientific judgments—formed the subject of an irate discussion. The objectivity of social science became the major victim when all those who so firmly believed in it found that they held opposing world views. (One must add here, however, that this was very much to the liking of those who do not share the faith in positivist methodology!)

If "schools make no difference"[13]—a statement directly opposed to operative American ideology—what, many asked, explains the social inequality between the races? Genetic factors[14] resulting in a meritocracy?[15] Too little "real," that is, nonthreatening integration (as opposed to formal integration)?[16] Or, simply, individual luck?[17] Whatever the scientific answers, interpretations, and suggested policy measures spun off from the discussion,[18] they have clearly revealed the ideological nature of the debate,† and, in their dissonance, have dealt a serious blow to a long-cherished part of the American myth.

Whatever else their differences, neopositivist social scientists tend to agree that the solution to social inequality lies more properly in the hands of administrators and public policy-makers. Marginal groups are objects of bureaucratic operationalizations and manipulative social measures—a view that flows directly from their acceptance of the methodology of quantitative empirical research in which it is an implicit assumption. This methodology tends to take

* Measured in terms of plant, formal curricula, and teaching quality.

† It is therefore not surprising that Daniel Bell in his defense of merit, achievement, and universalism as the principles of postindustrial society, prefers the findings of Jencks, i.e., that "luck" and "on-the-job competence" are largely responsible for economic success.[19]

into account only that which is measurable and overemphasizes static and *passive* characteristics of situations and persons. What is left out is that marginal groups, in their struggle for equality, may very well learn "that for the realization of the matter itself, a massive change of men is necessary, which on its part can only develop in a *praxis*-oriented movement, in a *revolution*; and that revolution is not only necessary, because the *ruling* class cannot be destroyed in any other way, but also because it is only through revolution that the *destroying* class can manage to get rid of all of its old dirt, and thus become enabled to found a new society."[20] In other words, the *object* social classifications of administrators and social scientists may well become irrelevant when the persons they have so categorized start to organize and act contrary to expectations.

The controversy about the Coleman report also highlights three other developments. First, it documents a trend both toward a scientification of political debate and a politicization of scientific discourse. Second, it introduced a new concept of equality which is also implicit in many of the demands of marginal groups for equal representation: Equality of result[21] projects a socialist ethic, according to which an unequal distribution of goods, if it were to occur, should only favor the disadvantaged.*[22] And third, it has called attention to the immense expansion of the state.

IV

The post-industrial society adds a new criterion to the definitions of base and access: Technical skill becomes a condition of operative power, and higher education the means of obtaining

---

* Daniel Bell rejects this new conception of "fairness" and "justice" as a possible foundation of postindustrial society, because, he argues, these values cannot be translated into operational terms, but more importantly, because postindustrial society, according to him, needs status differentials for persons with different levels of scientific and technical competence.[23] The major institutions of postindustrial society—"the institutions of science and scholarship, culture and learning"—must therefore in his view be exempted from democratic control. Bell's position on equality reveals once more his technocratic and meritocratic bent, though tempered with a measure of welfare democracy for those who fall into neither category. Bell does not bother to operationalize "competence" and "capability." His assessment of the university as a meritocratic institution is based on a dissociation of the university from the larger society. His views are thus an idealization and distortion of the present or a projection into the future.

technical skill ... technical competence becomes the overriding consideration ... Increasingly, the newer professional occupations, particularly engineering and economics, become central to the decisions of the society. The post-industrial society, in this dimension of its status and power, is the logical extension of the meritocracy; it is the codification of a new social order based in principle on the priority of educated talent.

(Daniel Bell, 1972)[24]

The full development of capital will occur ... when the whole production process will no longer be subsumed under the immediate skillfulnss of the worker but takes on the form of the technological application of science. To give production a scientific character is therefore the tendency of capital...

(Karl Marx, 1857–58)[25]

Since World War II, the United States has grown aware that in a world divided not only by national capitalist interests but also by a cold war between different political-economic systems, the potential for successful competition on the international market and political leverage would depend, more and more, on the tempo of scientific-technical innovation. Expenditures for research and development have soared exponentially since its beginnings in the New Deal era, the properties of scientifically and technically skilled manpower within the total labor force have rapidly increased, and the higher education system has been greatly expanded.[26] The bill for scientific-technical progress has generally been footed by the federal government, which has channeled vast funds into the military sector in order to maintain a superiority in the cold war and guarantee continued technical innovation. Government contracts have made the technically most advanced industries (aeronautics, electronics, armament- and space-technology, telecommunications) dependent on state support and at the same time the beneficiaries of increased size because of these state contracts.[27] The policies of the new "contract state" have had a variety of important structural effects. They have furthered the concentration, if not monopolization, of the economy.[28] The creation of complex weapons systems and modern technologies has necessitated the development of modern management, planning, and budgeting techniques on the part of both government and industry.[29] The Executive branch has been strengthened, although the fragmentation of governmental power

159

has not been effectively overcome. Thus, numerous federal agencies continue to compete for administrative decision-making powers, and despite attempts to develop some coordinated planning within individual sectors—i.e., the military, especially under McNamara[30]—or to increase cooperation among the different agencies, planning is still haphazard and partial.[31]

State investments in line with corporate interests have favored capital- and technology-intensive industries, notwithstanding the continued existence of a large reservoir of unskilled labor and the problems flowing from it. The astronomical sums spent on research and development, scientific and technical innovations, have further unbalanced the economic growth of the country by exacerbating the imbalance between large and small companies, between technology- and labor-intensive industries, and between different regions of the country in terms of economic investments and output, revenues, levels of human skills, educational and medical facilities, etc. In addition, these commitments have plunged the state into a fiscal crisis, with drastic effects on the public sector.[32] The state now not only subsidizes and guarantees the private profits of giant corporations, but also, as in the case of the military sector, it is the only buyer and consumer of the corporations' product. This means that the largest subsidies flow into economic nongrowth sectors which are publicly funded but privately exploited and whose technological contributions to the production of consumer goods are mere by-products at tremendous overcosts.[33] Consumer prices rarely benefit from technical innovations, because in their quasi-monopolistic position, corporations are free to "make" prices[34] and to set production "at a level which will maintain prices and acceptable profit margins in terms of costs, invested capital, and the attractiveness of corporate paper to investors."[35] In other words, new cost-saving techniques have often led to restricted production so as to avoid having to lower fixed prices. Technological innovations, of course, endanger the employment of the less skilled. Automation, once introduced, takes its toll slowly but steadily (cf. the so-called silent firings).[36] And, again it is the state that must pay much of the cost of retraining and upgrading the labor force or of unemployment compensation and welfare.[37]

160

By building its own production plants for technology-intensive sectors,[38] American corporate capitalism has used its technical and managerial predominance to expand its markets abroad. This process has gained momentum during the last few years, with the accelerated meshing of national expansion and the organization of multinational firms. U.S.-dominated multinational corporations have been attracted by the higher profit rates in foreign countries, and the U.S. has thus expanded its overseas markets even more. Under the current conditions of growing "national" competition on the world market (cf. Japan, European Common Market), the American government is faced with having to provide incentives (e.g., for the costs for the economic infrastructure such as transportation facilities, water, power, education, and research) to keep its corporations producing at home or to attract them to the underdeveloped regions within its continental boundaries. The "antisocial" costs of capital utilization by private corporations in the areas of ecology, welfare, urban renewal, and crime control, to mention just a few, burden federal as well as city and state budgets.[39]

In line with the multiplication of state functions and expenditures, government employment on the three levels of government has greatly increased (between 1950 and 1966 they had already grown by 25 percent).[40] Much of this expansion has been filled by professionals working in the fields of education, health, welfare, transportation, and police protection. Their work, for the most part, is mostly concerned with the human and social costs of modern capital accumulation. Having been trained in the university, and most of them for governmental service, they have internalized not only the ethics of public office, but also their respective professional ideology. Since their professional socialization at the university has been aimed at integration, they tend to be blind to the cost factor inherent in their work. The fiscal crisis of the state and the relative underdevelopment of the public sector, the intensifying and at times explosive pressures in public institutions (prisons, schools, colleges) have, however, recently started to undermine the loyalty which many of these professional public servants learned as students.*

If it is indeed true that the new social order of postindustrial

---

* Cf. the recent strikes by teachers and other public-service employees.

society rests in principle on the priority of educated talent, as Bell says, one has to point out also that this "educated talent" is being increasingly subsumed under the dictates of capital. To quote Marx: "To give production a scientific character is therefore the tendency of capital." This subsumption[41] of intellectual work, however, is not limited to production. It extends to all spheres of society (production, reproduction of labor, legitimations) and is also responsible for a reorganization of the class arrangements as well as the educational processes. The emergence of the multiversity with its hierarchical structure and the spreading of a technocratic ideology* are complementary to the growing scientific nature of production and the increasing state activities in the promotion of research and development. Historically, the new socioeconomic pressures within the colleges and universities first made themselves felt on a large scale during the sixties, and it was then that student protest developed across the nation.

V

Finally, the work of the intellectual always retains some of his unique subjectivity. In contrast to physical labor, which is characterized by repetition and divisibility, intellectual work contains a number of processes which are not reproducible.... The search for innovations cannot be directed from outside. In the same vein, intellectual work cannot be carried out indiscriminately by anybody.

(Serge Laurent, 1968)[43]

In our discussion of the social-scientific explanations of student protest we have analyzed in detail one aspect of the progressive subsumation of intellectual work, education, and knowledge under the conditions of advanced U.S. capitalism. That is, we found a trend toward an ahistorical, technocratic, and anticritical social science serving in the ideological defense of the system. But we also found that not all writers and scholars have lost their critical faculty.

Student protesters of the sixties and seventies were certainly not primarily concerned with the waning possibilities of developing and maintaining their creative potential and genuine intellectual needs;

* "We move toward a new era in which science can fulfill its creative promise and help bring into existence the happiest society the world has ever known" (President Kennedy, 1963).[42]

162

but intuitively or not, they did address themselves to this issue when they expressed their sense of alienation and frustration. Their alienation translated itself into explosive acts against competitive pressures, a disciplinary grading system, and a sterile and meaningless curriculum. Theirs was a bleak view of the future, which for many did not seem to hold the promise of creative work and intellectual challenge but only dependence on megabureaucracies. On the personal level, student protest against the deintellectualization induced by the changes of capitalism has taken on the form of a value-conflict—one between "humanistic" and "technocratic" values, for example—and on the group level, the form of organized group or class conflict.

Viewed from this perspective, the structural basis of the student protest has been a combination of a temporary marginality status and classlike conditions. Students are marginal to the increasingly classlike intellectuals because they are not yet part of that "class," but at the same time, while in the universities, they experience some of the tensions and pressures associated with their anticipated role and class position. The explanation for the almost complete disappearance of overt student protest at the present time is furnished in part by the absence of future high conflict potential resulting from an oversupply of university-trained manpower.

This is not to say that the student protesters of the sixties and seventies developed a fully articulated class politics. On the contrary, for a long time they were also concerned about "moral" issues—racism and imperialism—thereby promoting the traditional democratic ethos. While Vietnam and the black cause furthered and speeded up student mobilization, as solitary issues they seemed to have hampered the development of a political consciousness and the involvement in a genuinely radical politics. The escalating conflicts in the country during the sixties, however, as well as the student struggle itself, created a situation in which some students and intellectuals have learned to tie the various aspects of the crisis together. They have learned that their moral indignation about Vietnam, poverty, and racism, as well as their disaffection with and sadness about their student experiences and future prospects as intellectuals, are based on the same objective societal changes. They

163

have learned to break the mechanism of legitimation where societal conflicts manifest themselves in individually experienced tensions and are privatized and consequently resolved as personal problems. Some may even have become dimly aware that as members of a still relatively privileged stratum, they may serve their own interests best if they advocate radical change in the interest of the disadvantaged.

To return to our original concern—the possibilities of qualitative change—the question is under what conditions and to what extent student protest will continue, intensify, become radicalized, and perhaps spread to other intellectuals and scientists on whose loyal cooperation modern U. S. capitalism is becoming increasingly dependent. The answer is, perhaps, best put in the form of an assessment. The growing capitalist subsumption of intellectual work creates the following conditions: intellectuals as scientific workers in the sphere of production (e.g., in huge research laboratories or in many middle management positions,) experience their work increasingly as labor; this is especially true the more the division of labor and the development of hierarchical structures progress. As public employees, intellectuals experience not only the tensions resulting from the relative underdevelopment of this sphere (e.g., poor plant facilities, understaffing), but also pressures by organized marginal groups (e.g., welfare groups). As persons seeking to develop or cultivate their individuality, they resent the "dehumanization" of their education or work. Finally, their creativity and critical faculty, which are indispensable prerequisites of scientific-technological innovation, become the targets of an integrative socialization process which may easily provoke opposition and lead to an exploration of the "dangerous zones" of the system, for example, the questioning of the principle of the ethical neutrality of science.

On the other hand, this potential for dissent is counterbalanced by the hierarchical position of scientific workers in private and public industries and administrations, although there are more homogeneous intellectual groups, such as teachers. But the functional diversity of intellectuals keeps even them in a state of occupying erratic blocs. This lack of organization, as well as the current surplus of scientists, who cannot possibly be absorbed by the labor market, add further to the fragmentation of intellectuals. It

164

seems that solidarity is relatively most highly developed among public employees, many of whom are members of unions or associations. Faced with threats of possible unemployment, however, union members have tended to fall back on access and job-security procedures and fail to see their connection to political issues.

The academically trained are further fragmented by the difference in prestige accorded to degrees and academic institutions, so that the hierarchical differences in the educational sector reflect and help determine the social stratification of the larger society. For example, education at the less prestigious colleges tends to be instrumental and technocratic. Graduates of such institutions are more likely to fill lower-level and nonintellectual jobs. The enormous expansion of the higher-education system during the last decade has not led to better jobs for all graduates, but rather to a larger pool of *overqualified* labor, which in itself is an ingredient of potential unrest and dissent. Other ingredients are the "half-educated" or functionally miseducated, who, finding that their worthless degrees do not lead to upward social mobility, become aware of their role in the economic stabilization process.

If a political strategy of change is to exploit the above-mentioned disaffections, the traditional antiorganizational bias (the egotism aspect of individualism) of intellectuals would have to be redirected. Our analysis suggests that this is most likely to occur among persons whose motivation for protest is fed by more than one source (blacks, Puerto Ricans, women, etc.) and who have a nonintellectual constituency. Furthermore, it is most likely to happen in the public sector, in which marginal groups already exert organized pressures, though still primarily related to gaining access. It is in this sector that nonwhite and white intellectuals as well as the disadvantaged might learn that the unskilled and semiskilled cannot gain access to an economy geared to a technology-intensive industry because they cannot compete for highly qualified technical jobs. In other words, they may realize that poverty is created by this society and is an integral part of it. Thus, the public sector is the likely area for both marginal and intellectual groups to undergo a common political learning process. Another possible sphere for such a learning process

165

to develop may possibly reside in the multinational corporations.

VI

The question still remains whether intellectuals and marginals provide two distinct potentials for radical change. By discussing them one at a time we may have given the impression that they are indeed separate, with only tenuous connections. This impression would be both unfortunate and erroneous. Throughout our discussion we have been guided by our own admonition to devote attention to the method of presentation, but in so doing, we have also explored the interconnections between the two phenomena. The protest manifestations, occurring as and when they did, suggest the interrelatedness and common basis of these two groups. Despite the recent heraldings of an end to protest and dissent, there is evidence which points instead to a shift in tactics and in targets. The most obvious of these have been the attempts to use conventional means within established institutions, the use of the legal system and the courts for political redress, and the exposure of such counterproductive and brutalizing institutions as prisons and mental hospitals. In other words, rather than the disappearance of the "era of protest," we may now be witnessing a march of protest "through the institutions."* What remains to be tested, of course, is the relative strength of the march and the countermeasures of containment.

Some social scientists have, as we have shown, attempted to link the two protest-prone sectors. Theirs, however, has been an additive view. Their analysis departs from the assumption that students and marginal groups are distinct and quasi-autonomous "wholes" whose relations are only tactical and coincidental. Such reasoning is an integral part of the theoretical framework of most explanations of protest, permitting the location of protest potential to be shifted from one sector to another, depending on the most current and blatant confrontation, and is a theoretical perspective which supports the tautological reasoning that "something cannot be, because it is not supposed to be."

* This "program," first articulated by Rudi Dutschke, a West German student leader, has recently been discussed by Richard Flacks.[41]

166

What has been overlooked are the internal differentiations, fragmentations, and even schisms *within* the two groups. Since the internal conflicts that might arise in ascribed status groups are, in a certain sense, more easily recognized because of their closer ties to poverty and the peripheral sectors of the economy, let us use the case of the intellectuals briefly to summarize the importance of this oversight. We have suggested that within this group there is a growing polarization between critical intellectuals and technocrats. This bifurcation has come into sharp focus since the mid-century. Its development is connected with the clearer delineation of the classlike character of intellectuals as a group (their recruitment, for example, for the newer tasks called for by a highly sophisticated production). The murkiness of the holistic mechanical view has obscured the effects of this process on intellectuals, academics, and students, and, as a consequence has obfuscated the nature of internal class alignments and ideological differences taking place among them. On the other hand, if the smog covering this theoretical perspective is lifted, the phenomenon of technocratic apologists and the force of their ideological impact on the fragmentation of intellectuals become clear.

The still-elusive problem—even after having located, identified, explored, analyzed, and critically assessed it—is how in fact the "potential" is perceived and acted upon by the protagonists themselves. Recent revelations have brought into the open certain qualitative aspects of the radical potential as it appeared in 1968. Many Nixon supporters and close advisers perceived radical change to be an imminent threat, and for this reason, at least so they have testified, felt it necessary to engage in "radical" and illegal countermeasures. Critical students and marginal groups, while always aware of their "potential," if we are to believe their literature and their actions, perceived their strength to be one of a "state of becoming." That is, the movement saw itself as being in the process of clarification and structural organization. This self-perception reflects in part a problem long endemic to the American Left. But, in the context of the radical awareness in the sixties, the irresoluteness accompanying the state of becoming was a result of intraclass conflicts and the focus on intragroup identity by racial and other

167

ascribed-status groups. It is in regard to *perceived* potential that the ideological impact of the technocratic apologists played their most subtle and crucial roles. For they focused academic and intellectual thinking on the "naturalness" of the technocratic state in a democratic system, and used the prestige of their social-science expertise to convince both those in and out of government as well as those in and out of the movement that the search for group identity and the use of group power were but another form of good old-fashioned access politics. At the same time, they advocated a strong policy of governmental and institutional containment for those who broke the rules or questioned the stated limits of discourse. In the subtle ways in which "scientific" reasoning, policy advocacy, and influence on policy decision-making were combined to offset heightened political consciousness and realization of potential lies the meaning—and the provisional pay-off—of technocratic apologetics.

Notes

Notes to Chapter One

1. Cf. Karl Marx, *Grundrisse der Kritik der politischen Ökonomie* (Frankfurt/Main: Europäische Verlagsanstalt, n.d.), pp. 21ff. Also, Ernest Mandel, *Spätkapitalismus* (Frankfurt/Main: Suhrkamp Verlag, 1972), pp. 12ff.
2. For the concept of totality, *see* Marlis Krueger, "Sociology of Knowledge and Social Theory," *Berkeley Journal of Sociology* XIV, (1969), p. 158.
3. The relationship between "active participation" and "objectivity" has been widely discussed in the social-science literature. We share Karl Mannheim's view (developed in his *Ideology and Utopia* [International Library, 1936]) that objectivity can be increased by participation and even subjective involvement (*op. cit.*, pp. 44ff.)
4. See a survey reported by the *International Herald Tribune* on December 22, 1972, p. 3. Among many other sociological documentations of these characteristics, we recommend S. M. Miller and Pamela Roby, *The Future of Inequality* (New York: Basic Books, 1970).
5. Marlis Krueger and Baerbel Wallisch-Prinz, "Self Interpretations of German Intellectuals and the Experience of the Third Reich"; Paper for a conference at the Center for Inter-American Relations, New York, February 25, 1970, p. 1.
6. Peter L. Berger and Thomas Luckmann, *The Social Construction of Reality* (Garden City, N.Y.: Anchor Books, 1967), p. 126.
7. This conception was held by Karl Mannheim in his *Ideology and Utopia*, esp. chap. III.
8. The concept of the "socially unattached" or "free-floating" intelligentsia was taken over by Karl Mannheim, *op. cit.*, from Alfred Weber. Cf. Alfred Weber "Die Not der geistigen Arbeiter," *Die Krise des modernen Staatsgedankens in Europa* (Berlin, 1925), Part VI.
9. Cf. Seymour M. Lipset, *Political Man* (Garden City, N.Y.: Doubleday and Company, 1960), p. 333.
10. Cf. the German distinction between *"Kultur"* (culture) and *"Zivilisation"* (civilization), which was also introduced by Alfred Weber. Cf. also Krueger and Wallisch-Prinz, *op. cit.*, pp. 3 ff.
11. Cf. Harold Garfinkel, *Studies in Ethnomethodology* (Englewood Cliffs, N.J.: Prentice-Hall, 1968); Norman K. Denzin, "Symbolic Interactionism and Ethnomethodology: A Proposed Synthesis," *American Sociological Review*, XXXIV, No. 6 (December, 1969), 922–934.
12. George Herbert Mead, "The Nature of Scientific Knowledge", in A. Strauss

(ed.), *George Herbert Mead on Social Psychology* (Chicago: The University of Chicago Press, 1964), pp. 45ff.

13. For the following, *see* J. P. Nettl, "Ideas, Intellectuals, and Structures of Dissent," in Philip Rieff (ed.), *On Intellectuals* (Garden City: Anchor Books, 1970), pp. 57–134; Talcott Parsons, "The Intellectual: A Social Role Category," *ibid.*, pp. 3–26. In his attempt to locate intellectuals "in a profession, a role and an area of concern" (p. 90), Nettl rejects Parsons' definition of intellectuals "as the social role category whose incumbents tend to give primacy to cultural considerations over societal in the definition of their expectations and the obligations applying to them" (pp. 21–22) and instead suggests that one should approach the definition of intellectuals "from inside out, *from* certain types of ideas *toward* certain categories of idea-articulators" (p. 59). While Parsons focuses on the institutional differentiation and specialization of such idea-articulation in modern Western societies, Nettl considers the problem of "institutional location" to be primarily dependent "on types of ideas rather than types of people" (p. 59). Institutionalization may, at times, be inimical to the development of new ideas, he continues, while the Parsonian conception of an intellectual comfortably integrated into his society leaves us, in fact, with a devitalization of "the fundamental and necessary quality of intellect" (p. 59), i.e., the potential of dissent. According to him, Edgar Norin's definition remains the most usefull and acceptable to date. "The intellectual emerges from a cultural base and with a socio-political role [culture in this context is defined as a self-conscious concern with cultural dimensions]. ... Thus the intellectual can be defined from a triple set of dimensions: (1) a profession that is culturally validated, (2) a role that is socio-political, (3) a consciousness that relates to universals" (p. 88). Although Nettl sets out to focus on ideas, his final configuration is related more to persons than to ideas and their qualities.
14. Cf. Parsons' version of structural functionalism.
15. This position was held by Max Weber. For this and preceding note *see also* Krueger, "Sociology of Knowledge and Social Theory," pp. 159 ff.
16. Max Weber, *The Protestant Ethic and the Spirit of Capitalism* (New York: Charles Scribner's Sons, 1958), pp. 181 f. Weber seems to have conceived of such an automated system 46 years before Parsons.
17. Max Weber, "The Definitions of Sociology and of Social Action," in Talcott Parsons (ed.), *The Theory of Social and Economic Organization* (New York: The Free Press, 1968), pp. 88ff.
18. Lipset, *op. cit.*, p. 352. Nettl writes: "...the rise and sociological history of the American intellectual is in large part that of a butt and target of prevalent anti-intellectualism" (*op. cit*, p. 107).
19. Cf. Henry Elsner, Jr., *The Technocrats. Prophets of Automation* (Syracuse, N.Y.: Syracuse University Press, 1967).
20. Samuel Bowles, "Contradictions in Higher Education in the United States," in R. L. Edwards, M. Reich, T. E. Weisskopf (eds.), *The Capitalist System* (Englewood Cliffs, N.J.: Prentice-Hall, 1972), pp. 491–503.
21. Parsons, *op. cit.*, p. 21.
22. Cf. Lewis M. Killian, *The Impossible Revolution?* (New York: Random House, 1968).

170

23. Karl Marx, *Das Kapital*, I, *Marx-Engels Werke* (hereinafter *MEW*) (Berlin: Dietz Verlag, 1972), XXIII, 672–75. (Translated by Marlis Krueger.)

Notes to Chapter Two

1. Cf., e.g., Kenneth B. Clark, "The Civil Rights Movement: Momentum and Organization," in Talcott Parsons and Kenneth B. Clark (eds.), *The American Negro* (Boston: Houghton Mifflin, 1965), pp. 595–625.
2. Cf. Urban Research Corporation, *Student Protests 1969, Summary* (Chicago, 1970).
3. Cf. Ralph Turner, "The Public Perception of Protest," *American Sociological Review*, December, 1969.
4. Talcott Parsons, "Youth in the Context of American Society," in E. H. Eriksen (ed.), *The Challenge of Youth* (Garden City, N.Y.: Doubleday & Company, 1965), pp. 110–41 (first published in 1961 by The American Academy of Arts and Sciences).
5. Cf. Wolfgang Nitsch and Walter Weller (eds.), *Trends in Higher Education, Annotated Bibliography* (Paris-The Hague: Mouton, 1970).
6. Cf. e.g., Julian Foster, "Student Protest: What Is Known, What Is Said," in Julian Foster and Durward Long (eds.), *Protest: Student Activism in America* (New York: William Morrow & Co., 1970), pp. 27–58. Also, Kenneth Keniston: *Youth and Dissent* (New York: Harcourt Brace Jovanovich, 1972), pp. 369 ff.
7. We are aware of the problematic distinction between causal and functional explanations, because function and cause of a phenomenon are often confused. For a criticism, see George A. Theodorson, "The Use of Causation in Sociology," L. Gross (ed.), *Sociological Theory: Inquiries and Paradigms* (New York: Harper & Row, 1967), pp. 131–52.
8. Cf. Clarence Schrag, "Elements of Theoretical Analysis in Sociology," *ibid.*, pp. 220–53, esp. p. 224.
9. Richard C. Cornuelle, *Reclaiming the American Dream* (New York: Random House, 1965), p. 21.

Notes to Chapter Three

1. Cf. George F. Kennan, *Democracy and the Student Left* (New York: Bantam Books, 1968).
2. Kenneth Keniston, "The Sources of Student Dissent," *Journal of Social Issues*, XXIII (1967), 108–37. *See also* Richard L. Flacks, "The Liberated Generation: An Exploration of the Roots of Student Protest," *ibid.*, 52–75.
3. Cf. Herbert Hendin, "A Psychoanalyst Looks at Student Revolutionaries," *The New York Times Magazine*, January 17, 1971, pp. 16ff.
4. Cf. J. A. Paulsen, "College Student Behavior: Enigma or Dilemma?", *Journal of College Health* XIV (1965), 122–26.
5. Cf. Samuel Kaplan, "Revolt of an Elite," in Christopher G. Katope and Paul G. Zolbrod (eds.), *Beyond Berkeley: A Source Book in Student Values* (New York: Harper & Row, 1966), pp. 93–110.

6. Among those who subscribe to this view are E. H. Erikson, S. N. Eisenstadt, Talcott Parsons, Lewis Feuer, Paul Seabury, F. Solomon and J. A. Fishman. For a detailed discussion, see pp. 40–45.
7. It should be noted that some authors do recognize the limitations of their partial explanations. Cf., i.e., Hendin, *op. cit.*, p. 30.
8. Flacks, *op. cit.*, p. 62.
9. Keniston, *op. cit.*, here quoted from Walt Anderson (ed.), *The Age of Protest* (Pacific Palisades: Goodyear Publishing Co., 1970), p. 239.
10. Peter L. Berger and Richard J. Neuhaus, *Movement and Revolution* (Garden City, N.Y.: Anchor Books, 1970), pp. 78ff.
11. Peter L. and Brigitte Berger, "Will Blue-collar Offspring Be Running America?", *Boston Morning Globe*, February 23, 1971, p. 15.
12. Hendin, *op. cit.*, p. 28.
13. Kingsley Davis, "The Sociology of Parent-Youth Conflict," *American Sociological Review*, August, 1940, pp. 523–35.
14. See for example, Erik H. Erikson, "The Concept of Identity in Race Relations: Notes and Queries," in Talcott Parsons and Kenneth B. Clark (eds.), *The Negro American* (Boston: Houghton Mifflin, 1965), pp. 227–53. Also "Youth: Fidelity and Diversity," *The Challenge of Youth, op. cit.*, pp. 1–28.
15. S. N. Eisenstadt, *From Generation to Generation* (Glencoe: The Free Press, 1956).
16. Talcott Parsons, "Youth in the Context of American Society," in *The Challenge of Youth*, pp. 110–41.
17. Erikson, *Young Man Luther* (New York: W. W. Norton, 1958).
18. Cf. Lawrence F. Schiff, "The Obedient Rebels: A Study of College Conversions to Conservatism," *Journal of Social Issues*, XX (October, 1964), 74–95. J. A. Fishman and F. Solomon, "Youth and Social Action: An Introduction," I *ibid*, 1–27.
19. Fishman and Solomon, "Non-Violence in the South. A Psycho-social Study" (paper presented at the American Psychiatric Association's annual meeting in St. Louis, May, 1963; mimeographed); "Perspective on the Student Sit-in Movement," *American Journal of Orthopsychiatry*, XXXIII (October, 1963), 872–82; "Youth and Social Action. Action and Identity Formation of the First Sit-in Demonstration," II, *Journal of Social Issues*, XX, No. 1 (April, 1964), 36–45; "The Psychosocial Meaning of Nonviolence in Students Civil Rights Activities," *Psychiatry*, XXVII, No. 2 (May, 1964), 91–99.
20. Fishman and Solomon, "Introduction...," p. 7.
21. Fishman and Solomon, "Youth and...," p. 21.
22. *Ibid.*, p. 22.
23. *Ibid.*
24. Cf. the criticisms by David L. Westby and Richard G. Braungart, "The Alienation of Generations and Status Politics: Alternative Explanations of Student Political Activism," *Learning about Politics*, ed. by Roberta Sigel (New York: Random House, 1970), pp. 476–89.
25. Lewis S. Feuer, "Rebellion at Berkeley," *The New Leader*, XLVII (December, 1964).
26. Paul Seabury, "Student Freedom and the Republic of Scholars: Berlin and Berkeley," *Comparative Educational Review*, X, No. 2 (1966), 350–59.

27. Parsons, "Youth...," *op. cit.*
28. Talcott Parsons and Gerald Platt, "Age, Social Structure, and Socialization in Higher Education," *Sociology of Education*, XLIII, No. 1 (Winter, 1970), 1–37.
29. Cf. Daniel Bell, "Notes on the Post-industrial Society, I and II," *The Public Interest*, No. 6, Winter, 1967, pp. 24–35; and *ibid.*, No. 7, Spring, 1968, pp. 102–18.
30. Robert Coles, "Serpents and Doves: Non-violent Youth in the South," *The Challenge of Youth*, p. 256.
31. Christian Bay, "A Social Theory of Intellectual Development," in Nevitt Sanford (ed.), *The American College* (New York: John Wiley, 1967), p. 978.
32. Bay, "Political and Apolitical Students: Facts in Search of a Theory," *Journal of Social Issues*, XIII, No. 3 (July, 1967), 88.
33. Kenneth Keniston and Michael Lerner, "The Unholy Alliance Against the Campus," *The New York Times Magazine*, November 8, 1970, p. 86.
34. Cf. Jürgen Habermas, "Die Scheinrevolution und ihre Kinder," *Die Linke antwortet Jürgen Habermas* (Frankfurt/Main: Europäische Verlagsanstalt, 1968), pp. 5–15.

Notes to Chapter Four

1. Seymour M. Lipset, *Political Man* (Garden City, N.Y.: Doubleday & Company, 1960), p. 28.
2. Cf. Seymour M. Lipset and Philip G. Altbach, "Student Politics and Higher Education in the United States," in S. M. Lipset (ed.), *Student Politics* (New York: Basic Books, 1967), p. 202.
3. *Ibid.*, p. 201.
4. Philip G. Altbach, "Students and Politics," *Student Politics*, p. 82.
5. Cf. Kenneth Keniston, "The Sources of Student Discontent," in Walt Anderson (ed.), *The Age of Protest* (Pacific Palisades: Goodyear Publishing Co.), p. 239.
6. *Ibid.*, p. 230; Lipset and Altbach, *op. cit.*; Richard E. Petersen, "The Student Left in American Higher Education," in Lipset and Altbach (eds.), *Students in Revolt* (Boston: Beacon Press, 1970), pp. 202f.
7. Lipset and Altbach, "Student Politics...," pp. 215f, and Keniston, *op. cit.*
8. Sidney Hook, "Responsibility and Violence in the Academy," in Marvin R. Summers and Thomas E. Barth (eds.), *Law and Order in a Democratic Society* (Columbus, Ohio: Charles E. Merrill Publishing Company, 1970), p. 216.
9. Cf. Hook, *ibid.*, p. 217, and Talcott Parsons and Gerald Platt, "Age, Social Structure, and Socialization in Higher Education," *Sociology of Education*, XVIII, No. 1 (Winter, 1970), pp. 1–37.
10. Cf. Lipset, "American Student Activism, in Gary R. Weaver and James H. Weaver (eds.), *The University and Revolution* (Englewood, N.J.: Prentice-Hall, 1969), p. 28; Irving Kristol, "A Different Way to Structure the University," *Confrontation: The Student Rebellion and the Universities, op. cit.*, pp. 150–53; Irving Howe, "The Politics of Confrontation," in Irving Howe (ed.), *Student Activism* (Indianapolis: Bobbs-Merrill, 1967). An excerpt appears in Gregory Armstrong

(ed.), *Protest: Man Against Society* (New York: Bantam Book, 1969), pp. 161–68; Lewis Feuer, "Rebellion at Berkeley," *The New Leader*, XLVII, December, 1964.

11. Hook, *op. cit.*, p. 217.
12. Lipset and Altbach, "Student Politics...," *op. cit.*, p. 200.
13. For a discussion of the structural and ideological changes of the concept of the "public" as originally conceived by the liberal bourgeoisie, see Jürgen Habermas, *Strukturwandel der Öffentlickeit* (Neuwied: Luchterhand Verlag, 1965), and for the American scene, C. Wright Mills, "The Structure of Power in American Society," in Irving L. Horowitz (ed.), *Power, Politics and People: The Collected Essays of C. Wright Mills* (London: Oxford University Press, 1963). *Also see* Lipset, *Political Man*, particularly chap. 2.
14. Edward Shils, "The End of Ideology?" *Encounter*, V, November, 1955.
15. Daniel Bell, *The End of Ideology* (New York: The Free Press, 1960).
16. Bell, "The End of Ideology in the West," in Chaim I. Waxman (ed.), *The End of Ideology Debate* (New York: Clarion Book, 1968), p. 96.
17. Bell, *The End of Ideology*, p. 374.
18. Bell, "The End of Ideology in the West," p. 104.
19. Lipset, *Political Man*, p. 403.
20. Published under the title *The Uses of the University* (Cambridge, Mass.: Harvard University Press, 1963).
21. *Ibid.*, p. vi, Introduction.
22. Bell, "Notes on Post-Industrial Society, I and II," *The Public Interest*, No. 6, Winter, 1967, p. 28. *See* also his book *The Reforming of General Education: The Columbia College Experience in Its National Setting* (New York: Anchor Books, 1968).
23. "Notes on Post-Industrial Society," p. 29.
24. Kerr, *op. cit.*, p. 87.
25. *Ibid.*, p. 39.
26. *Ibid.*, p. 118.
27. *Ibid.*
28. *Ibid.*, p. 120.
29. Lipset, "The Politics of Academia" (unpublished paper for Conference on Intellectuals held in Jerusalem March 14–18, 1970), pp. 81f, and 85 ff.

Notes to Chapter Five

1. See, e.g., Clark Kerr *et al.*, *Industrialism and Industrial Man* (Cambridge, Mass.: Harvard University Press, 1960); John K. Galbraith, *The New Industrial State* (Boston: Houghton Mifflin, 1967); Daniel Bell, "Notes on Post-Industrial Society" I and II, *The Public Interest*, No. 6, Winter, 1967. Similar ideas have been expressed by Karl Mannheim, Helmuth Schelsky, Jacques Ellul, Talcott Parsons, and Seymour Martin Lipset.
2. Bell, *op. cit.*, p. 29.
3. See Bruno Bettelheim, "Obsolete Youth," *Encounter*, *23*, 2, pp. 29–43; see also, Z. K. Brzezinski, *Between Two Ages: America's Role in the Technotronic Era* (New York: Viking Press, 1970).

4. Peter Berger and Richard J. Neuhaus, *Movement and Revolution* (Garden City, N.Y.: Anchor Books, 1970).
5. Peter and Brigitte Berger, "Will Blue-collar Off-spring Be Running America?" *Boston Morning Globe*, February 23, 1971. See also Chapter 3, p. 38 and footnote 11.
6. Daniel Bell, "Columbia and the New Left," in Daniel Bell and Irving Kristol (eds.), *Confrontation. The Student Rebellion and the Universities* (New York: Basic Books, 1968), pp. 67–107; *see* also the "Introduction."
7. Cf. Peter Berger and Thomas Luckman, *The Construction of Social Reality* (Garden City, N.Y.: Anchor Books, 1967), pp. 18ff.
8. Herbert Marcuse, *One-Dimensional Man* (Boston: Beacon Press, 1964).
9. Cf. Theodor W. Adorno and Max Horkheimer, *Dialektik der Aufklärung* (Amsterdam: Querido Verlag, 1947).
10. Cf. in contrast, Marcuse's essay on "Philosophy and Critical Theory," *Negations* (Boston: Beacon Press, 1968).
11. *See* Wolfgang Haug, "Das 'Ganze' and das 'ganz' Andere,' " *Antworten an Marcuse* (Frankfurt/Main: Edition Suhrkamp, 1968). See also p. 31 n.
12. Marcuse, "Liberation from the Affluent Society," in David Cooper (ed.), *To Free A Generation: The Dialectics of Liberation* (New York: The Macmillan Company, 1969), p. 185.
13. Ibid., p. 189. See also his *An Essay on Liberation* (Boston: Beacon Press, 1968).
14. Marcuse, "Liberation ...," p. 187.
15. *Ibid.*, p. 188.
16. Marcuse, *Counterrevolution and Revolt* (Boston: Beacon Press, 1970).
17. See, for example, Jean Baker Miller, "On Women: New Political Directions for Women," *Social Policy,* II, No. 2 (July–August, 1971), 32ff. See also Notes 22 and 29.
18. *Ibid.*, p. 86.
19. Cf. Claus Offe, *Strukturprobleme des kapitalistischen Staates* (Frankfurt/Main: Edition Suhrkamp, 1972), esp. p. 13.
20. See, for example, the essays by Cardoso and Weffort, Garciá, Stavenhagen, Quijano, Casanova, Fernandes, Pinto, Jaguaribe, Michelena, in *America Latina. Ensayos de Interpretacion Sociologico-Politica* (Santiago de Chile: Editorial Universitaria, S.A., 1970). And, André Gunder Frank, *Capitalism and Under-development in Latin America* (New York: Monthly Review Press, 1967).
21. Greg Calvert and Carol Neiman, *A Disrupted History: The New Left and the New Capitalism* (New York: Random House, 1972).
22. In this context, the technical intelligentsia has been defined as the new bourgeoisie. See Manuel Brider, "Neue Arbeiterklasse oder neue Bourgeosie?" in Richard Vahrenkamp (ed.), (Frankfurt/Main: Edition Suhrkamp, 1973), pp. 188ff.
23. Cf. John and Margaret Rowntree, "Youth as a Class," *International Socialist Journal*, February 25, 1968.
24. Daniel Bell and Irving Kristol, "Introduction," *Confrontation*, p. ix.
25. See, for example, Calvert and Neiman, *op. cit.*; Jürgen Habermas, "Technology and Science as 'Ideology,' " *Toward a Rational Society* (Boston: Beacon Press, 1970), pp. 81ff, esp. 102ff.; Claus Offe, "Politische Herrschaft and Klassen-

strukturen," in Gisela Kress and Dieter Senghaas (eds.), *Politikwissenschaft* (Frankfurt/Main: Europäische Verlagsanstalt, 1969).
26. Alan Touraine, *The Post-Industrial Society* (New York: Random House, 1968).

Notes to Chapter Six

1. Charles Reich, *The Greening of America* (New York: Bantam Books, 1970), p. 2.
2. See especially our review of psychological and political explanations of student protest in Chapters 3 and 4.
3. Herbert Marshall McLuhan, *Understanding Media* (New York: McGraw-Hill, 1964).
4. Seymour L. Halleck, "Hypotheses of Student Unrest," *Protest*, ed. by Julian Foster and Durward Long (New York: William Morrow, 1970) pp. 105–122.
5. Henry Winthrop, "The Alienation of Post-Industrial Man," *Midwest Quarterly*, IX, 1968, 129.
6. Paul Goodman, "Anarchism and Revolution," *The Great Ideas Today, 1970* (Chicago: Encyclopedia Britannica, 1970).
7. Herbert Marcuse, "Remarks on a Redefinition of Culture," *Daedalus*, Winter, 1965, pp. 190–207.

Notes to Chapter Seven

1. See Chapter 3, note 19.
2. Ruth Searles and J. Allen Williams, Jr., "Negro College Students, Participation in Sit-Ins," *Social Forces*, XL (March, 1962), 215–20. *See also* Harry Edwards, *Black Students* (New York: The Free Press, 1970), pp. 14ff.
3. J. Orbell, "Protest Participation among Southern Negro College Students," *American Political Science Review*, No. 61, June, 1967, pp. 446–56; here p. 455. Orbell bases his study mainly on data gathered in 1962 by Donald R. Matthews and James W. Prothro. Cf. their *Negroes and the New Southern Politics* (New York: Harcourt, Brace & World, 1966). *See also* A. Geschwinder, "Social Structure and the Negro Revolt: An Examination of Some Hypotheses," *Social Forces*, December, 1964), 248–56.
4. Orbell, *op. cit.*
5. Anthony M. Orum and Amy W. Orum, "The Class and Status Bases of Negro Student Protest," *Social Science Quarterly*, XLIX (December, 1968), 521–33. Reprinted in Jack R. Van der Slik (ed.), *Black Conflict with White America* (Columbus, Ohio: Charles E. Merrill Publishing Co., 1970), pp. 197–211; here p. 198.
6. Cf. Searles and Williams, *op. cit.*
7. *Report of the National Advisory Committee on Civil Disorders* (1968). Portions of it were reprinted in Sethard Fisher (ed.), *Power and the Black Community* (New York: Random House, 1970). here esp. pp. 228–53.
8. W. E. Perkins and G. E. Higginson, "Black Students: Reformists or Revolutionaries?" in M. Aya and N. Miller (eds.), *The New American Revolution* (New York: The Free Press, 1971), pp. 195–222.

9. *Ibid.*, esp. pp. 198, 204, 208, 217, 220–22.
10. Michael W. Miles, *The Radical Probe* (New York: Atheneum, 1971).
11. Perkins and Higginson, *op. cit.*, p. 204.
12. *The Report of the President's Commission on Campus Unrest* (New York: Avon Books, 1971). The quote is a composite drawn from pp. 91, 93, 92–93.
13. Cf. Anne Braden, "The Southern Freedom Movement in Perspective," *Monthly Review Special Issue*, July–August, 1965.
14. Harold Cruse, *The Crisis of the Negro Intellectual* (New York: William Morrow & Co., 1967).
15. In the following section we have drawn on:
    Peter M. and Mort N. Bergman, *The Chronological History of the Negro in America* (New York: Mentor Books, 1969), p. 378.
    Oliver C. Cox, *Caste, Class and Race* (New York: Modern Reader Paperbacks, 1970).
    Cruse, *op. cit.*
    Philip S. Foner, *W. E. DuBois Speaks; Speeches and Addresses 1890–1919 and 1920–1963* (New York: Pathfinder Press, 1970).
    E. U. Essien-Udom, *Black Nationalism* (New York: Dell Publishing Co., 1964).
    Eugene D. Genovese. *The World the Slaveholders Made* (New York: Pantheon Books, 1969).
    Hugh Davis Graham and Ted Robert Gurr, *The History of Violence in America. A Report to the National Commission on the Causes and Prevention of Violence* (New York: Bantam Books, 1969).
    Miles, *op. cit.*
    Gerald Mullen, *Flight and Rebellion, Slave Resistance in Eighteenth-Century Virginia* (New York, 1972).
    The Report of the National Advisory Commission on Civil Disorders.
    The Report of the President's Commission on Campus Unrest.
    Eric Williams, *Capitalism and Slavery* (New York: Capricorn Books, 1966).
    See also, Selected bibliography for Chapter 9.
16. Bergman and Bergman, *op. cit.*, p. 378.
17. Hope, Marjorie, *The New Revolutionaries* (Boston: Little Brown, 1970), p. 261.

Notes to Chapter Eight

1. Cf. Antonio García, "La estructura social y el desarallo Latinoamericano," *America Latina. Ensayos de Interpretacion Sociologico-Politica* (Santiago de Chile: Editorial Universitaria, S.A., 1970), pp. 45–81, especially pp. 45–47, where García discusses the ideological distortions of bourgeois and orthodox Marxist social theories about Latin American development. Also, Eugene D. Genovese, "Marxian Interpretations of the Slave South," in Boston J. Bernstein (ed.), *Towards a New Past; Dissenting Essays in American History* (New York: Vintage Books, 1969), pp. 90–125, especially his discussion of Marxism and economic determinism, pp. 93–98.

177

Notes to Chapter Ten

1. Cf. Claus Offe, "Politische Herrschaft and Klassenstrukturen. Zur Analyse spätkapitalistischer Gesellschaftssysteme," Gisela Kress/Dieter Senghaas (ed.), *Politikwissenschaft* (Frankfurt/Main: Europäische Verlagsanstalt, 1969), pp. 155–89, especially pp. 180–82.

2. Stokely Carmichael and Charles V. Hamilton, *Black Power: The Politics of Liberation in America.* (New York: Random House, 1967).

3. Kenneth M. and Patricia Dolbeare, *American Ideologies: The Competing Political Beliefs of the 1970s.* (Chicago: Markham Publishing Company, 1971), p. 133.

4. Sylvester Bell, "Who's on the People's Side?" *The Black Panther*, August 30, 1969, p. 9.

5. Huey P. Newton, in *The Black Panther*, August 23, 1969.

6. See, e.g., Roger Vekemans, *La Marginalidad en America Latina: Un Ensayo de Conceptualizacion* (Santiago: Desal, 1969).

7. Lothar Hack, Wulf Krause, Ute Schmidt, Werner Wackutka, "Klassenlage und Interessenorientierung," *Zeitschrift für Soziologie*, I, No. 1 (January, 1972), 15–30, especially 26f.

8. See James O'Connor, "The Fiscal Crisis of the State, Part I," *Socialist Revolution*, I, 1970, 12ff; especially 43–47, and "The Fiscal Crisis of the State: Part II," *Socialist Revolution* II, 1971, 34ff.

9. Godfrey Hodgson, "Do Schools Make a Difference?," *The Atlantic*, CCXXXI, No. 3 (March, 1973), 35–46, here p. 36. On the same page, Hodgson writes: "Education has always seemed one of the most acceptable ways of using the national wealth to provide opportunity for the poor without offending the comfortable."

10. Hodgson rightly remarks that the NAACP "knew that education was so firmly associated with equality in the public mind that it would be an easier point of attack [i.e., against segregation] than, say, public accommodations or housing." *Ibid.*

11. See *ibid.*, p. 45. This is not to say that this controversy *caused* the cutbacks, which also were visited on public housing and welfare.

12. James S. Coleman, *Equality of Educational Opportunity* (Washington, D.C.: U.S. Government Printing Office, 1966).

13. S. M. Lipset's summary of Coleman's findings. Quoted by Hodgson, *op. cit.*, p. 35.

14. Arthur R. Jensen, "How Much Can We Boost IQ and Scholastic Achievement?" *Harvard Educational Review*, XXXIX, 1969, 1–123.

15. This problem has most recently been discussed by Daniel Bell, "On Meritocracy and Equality," *The Public Interest*, Fall, 1972, pp. 29–68, especially pp. 31–34.

16. David Cohen and Tom Pettigrew, *Racial Isolation in the Public Schools* (Washington, D.C.: U.S. Commission on Civil Rights, U.S. Government Printing Office, 1967).

17. Christopher Jencks *et al.*, *Inequality: A Reassessment of the Effect of Family and Schooling in America* (New York: Basic Books, 1972).

18. Moynihan, e.g., drew the conclusion that much had been achieved in the past

and that spending on schools should not increase beyond a necessary minimum. See Frederick Mosteller and Daniel Patrick Moynihan, *On Equality of Educational Opportunity* (New York: Random House, 1972). This book grew out of a Harvard seminar on the Coleman report. Jencks, *op. cit.*, on the other hand, is in favor of more spending, if only to make education more enjoyable.

19. Bell, *op. cit.*, especially pp. 42–43, and footnote 7 on pp. 47f.
20. Karl Marx and Friedrich Engels, *Die deutsche Ideologie*. MEW, III (Berlin: Dietz Verlag, 1969), 70. (Translated by Marlis Krueger. Authors' italics.)
21. See Daniel Bell's discussion of this concept in *op. cit.*, pp. 47ff.
22. See Jencks, *op. cit.*, and John Rawls, *A Theory of Justice* (Cambridge, Mass.: Harvard University Press, 1971).
23. See Daniel Bell, *op. cit.*, p. 65.
24. *Ibid.*, p. 41.
25. Karl Marx, *Grundrisse der Kritik der politischen Ökonomie* (Frankfurt/Main: Europäische Verlagsanstalt, based on the Moscow edition of 1939 and 1941), pp. 586 f. (Translated by Marlis Krueger.)
26. *See*, for example, H. L. Nieburg, *In the Name of Science* (rev. ed.; Chicago: Quadrangle Paperbacks, 1970), especially chapters III and IX; Joachim Hirsch, *Wissenschaftlich-technischer Fortschritt und politisches System* (Frankfurt/Main: Suhrkamp Verlag, 1970), especially pp. 100–106.
27. Nieburg, *Ibid.* Chapter IX; Hirsch, *Ibid.*, p. 103. James O'Connor, "The Fiscal Crisis of the State, Part I and Part II," *op. cit.*
28. Nieburg, *ibid.*, p. 191. Paul A. Baran and Paul M. Sweezy, *Monopoly Capital* (New York: Monthly Review Press, Modern Reader Paperback, 1966), pp. 92ff.
29. O'Connor, Part I, pp. 31ff; Hirsch, *op. cit.*, p. 103.
30. See Andrew Schonfield, *Modern Capitalism* (New York: Oxford University Press, 1965), p. 324.
31. Schonfield, *ibid.*, especially pp. 315–26. *See* also, Joachim Hirsch and Stephan Leibfried, *Materialien zur Wissenschafts- und Bildungspolitik* (Frankfurt/Main: Suhrkamp Verlag, 1971), pp. 13f.
32. O'Connor, Parts I and II, *op. cit.*
33. Nieburg, *op. cit.*, p. 78f.
34. Baran and Sweezy, *op. cit.*, pp. 53ff.
35. Nieburg, *op. cit.*, p. 65.
36. Ben B. Seligman, *Most Notorious Victory: Man in an Age of Automation* (New York: The Macmillan Company, 1966), pp. 211ff.; Seymour L. Wolfbein, "The Pace of Technological Change and the Factors Affecting it," Simon Marcson (ed.), *Automation, Alienation, and Anomie* (New York: Harper & Row, 1970), pp. 53–78, especially pp. 77f.
37. O'Connor, Part I, *op. cit.*, p. 45.
38. Hirsch, *op. cit.*, p. 104.
39. O'Connor, Part I, *op. cit.*, p. 35f.
40. O'Connor, Part I, *op. cit.*, p. 15.
41. Marx distinguished between the "formal" and "real" subsumption of work processes. The latter form affects the structure and organization of the work itself, while in the former case, capital "uses" the work process but leaves its

organization unchanged. When we speak of subsumption here, we refer to "real" subsumption in the Marxian sense. Cf. Karl Marx, *Resultate des unmittelbaren Produktionsprozesses* (Frankfurt/Main: 1968), p. 47f.

42. Excerpts from his address printed in *Science*, November 29, 1963, p. 1129. Here quoted from Nieburg, *op. cit.*, p. 75.

43. Serge Laurent, "Essai sur la situation de class des intellectuels," *Economie et Politique*, No. 172–73 (November–December, 1968), pp. 25–55; here p. 34. (Freely translated by Marlis Krueger.)

44. Richard Flacks, "On the New Working Class and Strategies for Social Change," in Philip G. Altbach and Robert S. Laufer (eds.), *The New Pilgrims: Youth Protest in Transition* (New York: David McKay Company, 1972), pp. 85–98.

Index of Names
and Authors

184

Webb, Beatrice, 7n.
Webb, Sidney, 7n.
Weber, Alfred, 169n.
Weber, Max, 15, 16, 170n.
Wechsler, James, 7n.
Weffort, Francisco C., 175n.
Weisskopf, T. E., 170n.
Weller, Walter, 171n.
Wellmer, Alfred, 7n.
Williams, Eric, 177n.

Williams, J. Allen, 176n.
Williams, William Appleman, 141n.
Winthrop, Henry, 77, 176n.
Wolfbein, Seymour L., 179n.
Wolfe, Thomas, 118
Wynn, Prathia Hall, 97

Yerby, Frank, 119

Zolbrod, Paul G., 171n.

Subject Index

status inconsistency (relative deprivation), 83–85
Bolshevik Revolution, 17, 114, 115
anti-Bolshevism, 114

Cambodian invasion, 27
choice, 14, 32
Christian conscience, 107
CIA (Central Intelligence Agency), 123, 126
CIO (Congress of Industrial Organization), 111n., 118
PAC (Political Action Committee), 118
city (urban), 95, 124, 125, 132
inner, 153, 155
City College of New York (CCNY), 5, 6
civil rights movement, 25, 26, 27, 85, 87, 89, 127, 149, 155
Civil War (American), 16n., 92, 108
class
and caste, 86
and ethnicity, 82
and ethnic stratification system, 101
and marginality status, 20, 22, 82, 123
and mobility, 109, 110, 111
and periphery, 19–20
and race, 20, 82
class analysis and racism, 149
class analysis and sexism, 149
class politics, 163
class struggle (conflict), 108, 145, 155n., 163, 167
elites
postindustrial, 133
technocratic, 136
cold war (warriors), 4, 122

Coleman report, 157, 158
colonial (colonists, colonizers), 103, 104
anti-colonialism, 104
Columbia University, 26
communism (communists), 115, 120, 126
and socialists, 17n.
Third International, 115
Congress for Cultural Freedom, 55n.
consciousness
ascribed status (marginal) groups, 140
discussed, 146–156
change of, 75, 79
international or revolutionary, 154
political, 111, 112, 140, 163, 168
politization of, 148
discussed, 154
prepolitization, stage of, 148
subversive potential of, 80
technocratic, 112
Constitution, U.S., 112
cultural explanations of student protest
discussed, 73–80
instinctual liberation, 77, 78
mass media, 76, 77
postindustrial culture, 77
youth culture, 79

Declaration of Independence, 107, 112
dehistoricalization, 86, 100, 112
delegitimation, 152
democratic ethos, 3, 105, 106, 108, 112, 113, 114, 119, 122, 130, 138, 139, 163

Democratic Party, 28, 131, 138, 139, 140

democratic pluralism, 37, 120, 126, 127, 134, 136, 137
see also political explanations

dependency theory, 68

depolitization, 110, 111, 123

determinism
critical discussion of, 21, 102, 177n.
rejection of, 154

dialectic
of liberation, 67
of reform and revolution, 33, 155–156
see also access politics

dialectical approach, 32

Dred Scott decision, 93

dissent
political in America, 15, 16
Left, 116, 118, 119, 133
Right, 120, 121, 133

economic growth, 13, 18, 159–161
see also science and technology

economic explanations of student protest, 63–72
new working class thesis, 69
Neomarxian, 66–71
non-Marxist, 63–66
peripheral theory, 67–68
postindustrial society, theory of, 64–65

education, 108, 109, 114, 125, 130, 165
and upward mobility, discussed, 156–158
and postindustrial society, 161–162
see also multiversity, university

Emancipation Proclamation, 93

end of ideology, 127, 128, 135, 137
theory of, 55–58
see also political explanations

Enlightment, 104, 106

escapism, 116, 123

epistomology
social sciences, difficulty of, 8, 31–32

equality (equity), i, 4, 5, 6, 104, 108, 113, 131
of opportunity, 132, 157
of result, 132, 158

ethnicity
manipulation of, 81
ethnic stratification system, 101
see also class

FBI (Federal Bureau of Investigation), 123, 126

Federal Theater Project, 119

First International, 16n.

FSM (Free Speech Movement), 26

Freedmen's Bureau, 93

Fourierists, 16n.

generation gap thesis, 74
see also psychological explanations

ghetto, 95, 96, 124
see also slum

Great Depression, 17, 63, 95, 96, 110, 121, 128

Great Refusal, 78, 135, 135n.

Great Society programs, 128, 129, 130, 131, 132, 139

group
access, 111
identity, 132
solidarity, 110

189

Coordinating Committee), 25, 26, 29, 33, 86
slum, 96, 134
Socialism, 7n., 111, 116, 129
society
    crises of, 13
    spheres of, 13
    as totality, 8, 9
sociology
    critical, 6
    Frankfurt School, 7n., 30n., 31n., 66, 68
    Marxian analysis, 7
    positivistic, 6, 7, 10
    tradition of, 6–7
South, 25, 85, 91, 92, 93, 95, 120, 124, 139, 156
Southern plantation system, 91, 92
state
    expansion of, 158, 161
    expenditures of, 159–161
    fiscal crisis of, 160, 161
    function of, 145, 152, 159–161
    as employers of professionals, 15
    technocratic, 168
suburb, suburbanites
    see migration, city
subjugation
    of marginals, 22
    of professional class among blacks, 87
subsumption
    formal, 179–180
    real, 179–180
    of education (intellectual work, etc.), 13, 21–22, 87, 162, 164
    of production process, 159
syndicalism, 79, 115
system

crises of, 145–146
crisis management, 145–146
technical advances (innovation, know-how), 112, 132, 135, 137
technocratic, 112, 128, 134
    definition of, 13–14, 15
    apologists, 15, 113, 167
    culture, 4, 112, 136
    education, 165
    specialists, 15
    style, 129
Technocratic Party, 17, 117
technology
    animated, 77
    see also science
Third World, 132, 154
totality, 6n., 7
    societal, and directly experienced needs, 148, 163–164
    unity of scientific and historical process, 31
trade-unionism, 16n., 110, 115
    see also AFL, CIO
Transcendentalists, 16n.
TVA (Tennessee Valley Authority), 117

United Front, 119
university
    as locus of dissent, ii, 18, 113
    new function (importance) of, 58–60, 136
    role in society, 70–71, 109
    see also education, multiversity, science
University of California at Berkeley, 26, 29
Universal Negro Improvement Association, 94
urbanization